BEYOND THE SEA

GOLDEN SANDS

John T. Eber Sr.
MANAGING EDITOR

A publication of

Eber & Wein Publishing
Pennsylvania

Library of Congress
Cataloging in Publication Data

ISBN 978-1-60880-430-6

Proudly manufactured in the United States of America by

Eber & Wein Publishing

Pennsylvania

A Note from the Editor . . .

But we'll never do aught, I know, unless
 We are brave as our sires of old,
And face like them the bitterness
 Of the battle and storm and cold;
Unless we boldly stand,
 When men would hold us back,
With the helm-board in our hand,
 And our eyes to the shining track
  Of what may be
  Beyond the sea.

—Frederick George Scott
from "Knowledge" (1887)

Welcome, poets and readers. Over the past year I have diligently read your work, seen your joy, and felt your pain. I'm not alone in that experience for here we meet together again, between these covers, where we may run free and speak words dearest to us. Some of us obscure our identities, but we all bare our souls in these humble pages.

We are from all walks of life and we come together here to share with mutual respect our creations from beginners to seasoned veterans. Poets write about life gained and life lost, tragedies, outrage, transitions recognized, seasons celebrated, a year's worth of holidays, prescriptions for change, advice for the future, dreams, wonderlands, landscapes of melancholy, new love, old love, crushing heartbreak, creatures fair and ferocious, childhood memories, lifelong pursuits, and passionate spirituality. No topic is off-limits or ignored.

Life is sometimes cold, mechanical, and unforgiving, but we have love, art, and poetry to emancipate our spirits. Beauty woven with language can reconnect us with those we've lost. Verse can ring out the adoration we feel deep inside. Poetry can be a manifestation of playful, carefree whimsy. This beauty hides in all of us and takes a multitude of forms. Some poets exercise careful structure in their work while others employ a more organic composition. Rhyming or not, poems capture language as a living entity and give simple printed words vivacious energy.

Above all, this book is a record, a time capsule even, in which we can revisit the past, dream about the future, and reach our children's children. Verse has waned in public opinion, perhaps with the elevated pace of modern life, but its importance is still as vital, and it is here we take up that meaningful work.

Poetry permits us to tell our stories, heal from our pain, and celebrate our successes; it is a vital form of communication, a necessity of the human condition. The task does not always come easy, and may require the bravery Frederick George Scott describes above, but the reward is release, relief, and accomplishment. The same can be said for reading, too; can a story be told if no one hears it? Poetry is a hallowed covenant between writer and reader—one cannot exist without the other. Writers must read as much as readers need to venture out with their own voice.

Thank you, steadfast readers, and thank you, poets—I extend my deepest appreciation to all for keeping poetry alive and opening your hearts and confiding your experiences from which we may all learn and grow. Look with me now, beyond the sea, to what new adventures we will brave! May your pen always flow swiftly across the page. You have made history.

Desiree Halkyer
Editor

My Waterfall Remains

The pillow should've removed its tracks of tears by eight,
and made them all gone.
Instead the ninth hour showered a never-ending pond,

the pond would overflow and have its very own way,
soaking the pillow out of control
and creating for itself this lake.

At ten, the lake cried out for the ocean to join in,
the pillow conceded to the ocean and river for she knew;
it was a win, win.

By the eleventh hour the tears just refused to stop,
everything within just flooded out...
And I prayed for a "waterfall drought"...

In the twelfth hour the wetlands bring no shame,
the pond joined the lake, ocean, and river,
causing a massive overflow of rain,
...even
"The fountains also of the deep and the windows of heaven
were stopped and the rain from heaven was restrained"
(Genesis 8: 2 KJV).
But... my waterfall remains.

Reneé Drummond-Brown
Pittsburgh, PA

I, Reneé Drummond-Brown, am the wife of Cardell Nino Brown Sr. and from our union came Cardell Jr., Renee and Raven Brown. I am the offspring of Mr. and Mrs. Peter C. Drummond of Pittsburgh, Pennsylvania. My siblings are Delbert Drummond and the late Pastor Shawn Drummond. I was born in North Carolina, at Camp Lejeune US Naval Hospital. I am a graduate of Geneva College of Pennsylvania, and my love for creative writing is undoubtedly displayed through my very unique style of poetry. My poetry is inspired by God and Dr. Maya Angelou. Because of them I pledge this: "Still I write, I write, and I'll write!" Renee's poems with wings are words in flight can be seen at www.reneespoems.com.

The Poetry Contest

A poetry contest will sound distressed to some kids but I will try my best to impress whoever is reading this.
I know nothing about poetry I'm just trying to rhyme my words perfectly,
twenty-five thousand dollars is a lot of money for anybody,
most people will buy drugs or go out and not care about being litterbugs,
people get greedy and only worry about themselves when they have too much money.
The kids that don't have much and ignored or get punched deserve to be known and not alone,
I could buy a bigger house for my family they always wanted an upstairs to seem like millionaires,
or I could buy a car to get me far for my opportunities that will come in different countries.
I dream of a bigger world where the kids like me are more known,
my life is not so bad now but I'm still really sad about the past that went by too fast.
I'll donate to the poor and the ghetto everyone should have a chance to have something they own and can finance.
We let a piece of paper control us, trees die everyday because we don't care about the weight that follows us, the world as we know it is turning wickedly without the right faculty.
I just want a chance to set an example and make the sad and poor kids not so bashful,
Would you rather give it to someone with no morals or give it to a person with good sense in principles?
My dream would come true and I might get some self-esteem if you let me have a chance to be me.
I wouldn't even change the way I dressed I would just make people feel blessed.
Thank you guys for reading, I hope you change somebody's life and make something remembering.

Tatum Niemeyer
Catoosa, OK

Perfect Imperfections

A silly subject to pen,
Oblong circles, triangular squares,
Straight wavy lines,
One dot, one dash, single pairs?

Farewell hellos, alone togethers,
Forever nevers, silent sounds,
Middle ends, negative positives,
Sour sweets, square rounds.

In front behind, upside overs,
Inside outers, forward backs,
Blind sights, complicated simples,
Indigent millionaires, white blacks.

Light heavies, wrinkle smoothies,
Messy cleans, thick slenders,
Tall shorts, starched softness,
Downward ups, straight benders.

A silly subject to pen,
Perfect Imperfections,
Confuse a gifted mind
Was my intentions.

Doris Reifschneider
Scottsbluff, NE

I was born March 15, 1937 and have three brothers and one twin sister. Real feelings, humor, mystery, crying followed by laughter, and defeat followed by victory are my guidelines for a happy and satisfied life. God is my favorite critic, He understands me.

Untitled

I sit here looking through my tears, thinking of the past
Those silly days of childhood, too bad they couldn't last...
I was little, he was big (a giant in my eyes), he'd oft sit
Beside my bed till sleep would weight his eyes.

Then we grew up, he had to leave "for life was marching on";
I stayed behind to grow some more, he sang the Naval song.
Husband, father, officer, friend, were titles that he claimed
And I felt lost along the years and often cried in pain.

Now I'm not so little, you're not so big (still the giant in my eyes)
And I'll take my place beside your bed till angels close your eyes,
For you must leave and I must stay and take care of the others—
I love you so, I always will, my giant, my big brother.

Linda Baker
Burlington, IA

Freedom

In a world filled with hatred,
freedom is not just a word,
but something as a nation, we procure.

We stand together in unity,
overcoming every obstacle,
bringing to their knees every foe.

Tho' they bomb us, tho' they plot,
to destroy us, to some way bring us down,
we will be the victor.

This nation founded, on courage.
Until time is no more,
we always will prevail.

We will withstand every storm,
and peace we shall win,
together as one, always, until the end.

Chaerlagh O'Browning
Lexington, KY

I was born the son of a tenant farmer. We came from Siebloaw Mountains about seven kilometers south of Dublin, Ireland. I lost my one and only dodai, *meaning my only true love and beloved one, at fourteen. I have always been a hopeless romantic; I love to write romantic love poems though I no longer believe in love anymore. My given name was Charlemayne Alacoanin Doglas MacArthur O'Briensingerzweigerstonecyphers! So naturally we had to change our name, I became Chaerlagh O'Browning. I have a poem called "Yours Eternally." I was going to write to my beloved, I never have written it, because I have never found another true love. I hope to someday find another true love and write that song and poem yours eternally.*

Peace Offering

If I had some diamond rings
I would give a ring to you
If I had a fishing net
I would catch some fish for you

If you had a difficult job to do
I would finish it just for you
If I had a lot of gold
I would share some gold with you

If I had some strength to give
To lend a helping hand
I would give my arm to the Lord
And share His love throughout the land

If I had some time to think about
All the wonderful things Jesus did
I would learn about all of the miracles
And all the people that He saved

Gifts were to be given on
The twenty-fifth of December
Gold and myrrh were offered to Him
Just in case you cannot remember

It was their way of praising God
For His Son Jesus Christ was born
It was in Bethlehem He was laid
A "peace offering" had been made

Manny Alcantara
Gainesville, FL

Voyage of the USS Oriskany CV34 to Northern Italy

La Spezias Mountains reaching to the sky,
Her harbor which my ship now lies.
Her green valleys and salt sprayed shores,
A beauty I have not seen before.
Cities of Pisa and Florence are nearby too,
Bus trips to these cities are taken by some of the crew.
These were the smart ones by far; others went to the nearest bar.
We head to Naples called Napoli on a beautiful bay; Pompeii and the Isle of
Capri with its outside cafes and shops and the Church of San Michele with
The tile floors depicting Adam and Eve.
Pompeii at the foot of Mount Vesuvius must have been quite a town before
The volcano erupted and lava mummified many as they stood around.
Some businesses in Pompeii had murals of what we would call "porn," not
Too many clothes were worn.
The bus ride from Naples to Sorrento along the cliffs of the ocean blue, while
The bus driver sang and took in the view. We prayed we wouldn't go over
The side because the road wasn't really that wide.
Sailors lined up in white, excited to go ashore, on tours to Milan,
Venice, Genoa and Rome to explore.
Our next port was the best of all: Cannes on the French Riviera,
the bikinis were the smallest I seem to recall.

Charles Rodriguez
West Palm Beach, FL

I was born in the Williamsburg section of Brooklyn and went into the Navy at a young age. I started writing poetry on my first ship, the USS Shea DM: thirty poems about life at sea. One storm off Cape Hatteras did more damage than the war. After I was discharged, I returned to high school to receive my diploma. I re-enlisted in 1950 and was assigned to the Oriskany Shake Down Cruise to the Mediterranean and wrote poetry again. This was followed by South American ports around Cape Horn to West Coast, Asiatic Ports and Korean War. I was discharged in 1954, then married Jean Domanico, from Long Island, and we have five children and a large family. I worked twenty-four years for Grumman Aerospace and retired as senior analyst. I retired to West Palm Beach, FL.

Over the Sea and into the Blue

Over the sea and into the blue,
What a beautiful day as I'm thinking of you.
With the sun so bright and warm and new,
The clouds passing by with that subtle morning hue,
I can't help to think, not once but twice,
How lucky I am that you're in my life.
I think of all the special times we've shared,
Together just you and I,
Here and there and there again,
It's all very good I say with a grin.
For who would I rather be with than you,
Sitting next to each other on top of the moon.
I never felt so lucky or blessed I say,
To know we're together to share each new day.
Your smile, your charm and your sexiness too,
Just adds to the way that you move and you groove.
So this is a testament to the person I love,
That I praise and praise each passing new day,
That I share my life with in so many ways,
How I love you now and forevermore,
And forevermore I will always adore,
As I look over the sea and into the blue,
What a beautiful day it's been just thinking of you.

Roy R. Stone
Tampa, FL

My name is Roy Stone. I am an artist and choreographer teacher of ballroom, Latin and theatrical dance for thirty-six years. I am also a closet case singer and songwriter, and now, through your kindness, a poet. My inspiration for this pleasure that one may call poetry was someone that took me forty years to meet, a person filled with great kindness, strength, extremely intelligent, and so much love to give. I once thought I wanted all the riches the world had to give and I now realize through this poem that I am rich beyond imagination.

I Wanted to Tell You Everything

I wanted to tell you how often I cried.
How it was the only way I could fall asleep,
staining my pillow with thoughts of you.
How I wandered through my days barely alive,
fixing on my smile before I left and trying to keep it in place.
I wanted to tell you how I visited you every Sunday,
like a religion,
putting my ear to the ground.
But I couldn't hear you through the dirt.
How I brought you flowers, but they died too,
and everything dies, so why haven't I?
I wanted to tell you that life is colorless without you,
and my favorite color was always red.
How the sun is dull and everything turns to ash in my mouth.
I wanted to tell you, but how could I now that dust is dust again?
Now that dust is dust and you're never coming back.
I wanted to tell you everything.

Bethany Taylor
Cramerton, NC

Mother Nature

Last night I heard Mother Nature call
Telling all the leaves, it's time to fall
Then she whispered to the trees
It's time to send a winter freeze

She told Jack Frost to do his art
And warned the birds to depart
She advised Mother Rabbit and her brood
To plenish their home with lots of food

Be cautious, she told the doe and fawn
For hunters come in the early dawn
Find a good home, she told the bear
One that can take the winter's wear

Mother Nature does her deed
And all of nature taketh heed
She'll play tricks just like a con
Then start over when winter's gone

Linda L. Moore
Ames, IA

Longing to Love

The minutes passed as slowly as a snail by the sea
The hours and days were like eternity
But that time was coming when I would see you at last
As I waited and waited for the time to pass
Then at last the day came
The day I would speak your name
And say to you my darling my dear
How I've waited to have you so near
I would hold you and hug you like never before
And then I would kiss you because it is you I adore
Your lips are like fire, your cheeks they are red
You're a bundle of beauty from your toes to your head
Your hair sparkles like the sun on the dew
Your eyes glisten bringing out the beauty in you
Finally there is your wonderful smile
That makes you more beautiful than the Queen of the Nile

Walter P. Mazarick
Raleigh, NC

Remembrance

I used some 3-in-1 oil today.
Had to fix a rusted gate latch.
Bought this oil some 20 years ago.
Reminded me of my dad.
A can was always on his work bench.
I miss my dad,
All of my family who have passed away.
I look now to a cloud-filled sky and remember them,
Their love, their lives, their joys.
Can eternity be somewhere there beyond this infinite sky?
Will we meet again one day in some timeless realm?
I'd like to trust one day we will,
Though I cannot say for sure.
Yet certainly I know their presence here and now,
Infused within and through my soul.
These days they dwell within my mind,
In unaccountable, bittersweet moments of time
When God is kind.

Nick Lehnert
Longmont, CO

November's Angel

I've come to the end of
Another day
And I sit here all alone,
Thinking of you my darling
Up there in your heavenly home.

Only two years ago it has been;
"Seems like I can't forget,"
Only a moment I held you
But I remember that joy yet.

Just why I couldn't keep you
I cannot understand
But I know someday I'll meet you
If I obey my Christ's command.

If you were only here tonight
Two years old you would be.
We would celebrate your birthday—
Your daddy, you, and me.

Perhaps I should not question
The doings of my God,
But oh how awful it was dear
To put you beneath the sod.

For you, I went down into that valley
Which all mothers have to face
And I'd gladly go again dear,
For another to take your place.

Lana J. Rush
Lakeville, OH

In loving memory of dear Aunt Florence who lost a precious baby girl in November, 1927. Even though she could not have any more children of her own, she was a mother and confidant to many.

Drought

The ground so dry, huge cracks appear, up and down each row,
of crops that needed moisture bad, if they were thought to grow.
For weeks the sun had shone from high, drying nature's crust,
of earth and ditches once filled full, now turning them to dust.

An old man stood, with hands on hips, he gazed at his domain,
he raised his eyes toward Heaven, and said a silent prayer for rain.
"Dear Lord," he said, while looking up, tears swelled in his eyes,
"please open up the clouds above, let rain fall from the skies."

Across the fields another man walked behind his plow,
which once had glided through the soil, but hardly pierced it now.
He stopped his team, then wiped his brow, and slowly looked about,
eyeing nature's striking blow, the devastating drought.

His once proud crop, so tall and green, was now a mass of weed,
too dry to live, to live to die, on which the insects feed.
He worried of fire, in every drought, a chance for the starting flame,
to burn the fields which had been parched, by lack of needed rain.

As increased winds stir cross the field, he turns his head in wonder,
he heard a noise that sounds to him, like the distant roar of thunder.
His heart beats fast, he strains his ear, searching for a sound,
that tells of clouds to block the sun, and rain to cool the ground.

But no rains came, the drought went on, the crops all died of
thirst,
proving that by words of law, nature speaks hers first.
The loss is done, the farmers know, they have no drought to fear,
until they plant another crop, another time next year.

Robert W. Jones
Drakes Branch, VA

The Man

I've seen a man on a busy city sidewalk
Looked at his phone
Did not see the crack sticking out of the ground
Tripped and fell and got up
The slightest bit mad that no one helped
Kept walking
Ignores the overturned trash can to his left
Same with the homeless man with the tin cup
Walks into a office building
For a brief moment I cannot see the man
The man comes out yelling
Hails a cab

Ben C. Wolfe
Malvern, PA

Winter's Beauty or Beast?

We are as the craggy icicles of winter,
Nature's chandeliers for a time hanging firmly yet moored tentatively until winter's finale,
Casting a rainbow hue or casting a glacial blue,
Bestowing a curious prism or bestowing a cold pallor.
This is winter's mirror of mankind.
Admire or beware!

Marsha L. Cleversey
Merrimac, MA

Complete Man

I wish I could tell them the truth
But how do I explain
Something so complex
It first takes driving one insane
To feel all the emotions
For a man to be broken
And yet through it all a man still hoping
Nothing comes easy and it's not easily explained
Since day one we've given perceptions
All of the same thing
To begin to understand, one in which is a complete man
Something so complex as being a man
A man whom has followed his heart
And round and round he's gone down the drain
Something so complex
Will we ever begin to understand?
Like a seed that has fallen
Just to find his individual self
Like a seed that has sprouted
Just to find his social self
Nature and nurture
It works hand in hand
Two sides of the same coin
Just to find a complete man

Jarrid A. Glisson
Sylvania, GA

He's Lucky to Be Alive

The night brought back the pain,
which I'd thought had been gone,
when he'd said he'd change.
He knew, he said, he'd brought me pain.

Which I'd thought had been gone,
his addictions fought and pushed back.
He knew, he'd said, he'd brought me pain.
After so many years, it still reigned.

His addictions fought and pushed back,
time and time again, and I lived.
After so many years, it still reigned.
He's lucky to be alive.

Time and time again, and I lived
through it all, with broken promises.
He's lucky to be alive.
I've feared lately, that he'd die.

Through it all, with broken promises,
he's still alive to try again.
I've feared lately, that he'd die.
Only God keeps me alive.

Olivia Serena Snead
Philadelphia, PA

I Miss You

I miss you,
But you've never even met me.
What happened to the you that everybody loved,
So happy and carefree?
You were changed by society against your will.
The person you've become is a living catastrophe.

I'm scared of you.
You keep saying you hear voices.
So to block them out you crank the radio
Or make obscene noises.

You smile with tears streaming down your cheeks.
I look down and see a blood-stained sleeve.
I reach out to aid you...
But you scream at me to leave.

Society says you do this for attention.
It doesn't realize they pushed you to it.
Setting unrealistic standards to be met,
They all think what you do is a skit.

Then they look at me, beginning the same harassment.
I keep my guard up, saying, "Can't you see?
That this missing person I speak of...
Is me?"

Allison Leona Handley
Gilbert, AZ

Realization

Dusk is coming as quickly as I saw you,
I still haven't figured it out.
Are you the same man who broke my heart years back?
Is my mind just clouded?

The sky darkens and yet your light shines over me,
though you don't notice.
I am standing out of sight, but finding a way to see you,
with my eyes and soul.

You are so familiar but I don't trust what I know,
we seem to have met before but I can't remember.
That was a wonderful time of love and trust.
I know you are not the man from years back,
you are from before this life.
You are here now and you are eternal.

Lori K. Petrie
Fond Du Lac, WI

The Passing Love

In the pain so raw we found
A pleasure excruciating and pure.
A passing love that braced us then
The suffering to endure.

Drawn to its own, reflection of same
Insulated within, from without,
Held for a time from the rest of the world
Unmoved by concerns from about.

For common cause, time stood still,
In unison staving off proof,
The rearing glimpses all eclipsed
Our complicit denial of truth.

Subdued for few,
The persistent voice came knocking with ghosts from the past.
But now we stand defeated and worn,
Reality victorious at last.

Clare Morrison Mountfort
Fairfax, VA

Christmas Glow

Just before Christmas gentle snow
falls from the wintry sky;
The first covering, all aglow,
beautiful to every eye.

Each snowflake, a pattern unique,
amazing by design,
Silently descending...
miraculous... sublime.

Advent of the Son of God
is more amazing still.
Christ left Heaven's splendor
to do the Father's will.

Pure, sinless Lamb of God,
whiter than the snow,
Light of heaven descending—
the first Christmas glow.

Richard A. Murray
Fraser, MI

Our winters in Michigan are an opportunity to look beyond shoveling snow in sub-zero temperatures. My goal is to capsulize the parallel of God's spiritual purpose with His handiwork revealed. My wife, our three grown children, and our eight grandchildren have all given me inspiration for stories as well as poetry. I enjoy writing for them.

The Hardest Part

What's the point of being with someone,
you know is not the one?
Forcing yourself to have feelings that in reality do not exist.
Convincing yourself, you are in love.
When the person you truly love
is in love with someone else.
Patiently awaiting the moment of acceptance.
The moment in which the feelings become mutual.
While momentarily settling for "good" or "okay."

Everytime you kiss,
your heart is somewhere else.
Your mind wanders
to the pink pale lips that you desire.
The dark luscious hair you want to brush your fingers through.
Holding your feelings in to save the friendship that still exists.

But the hardest part is not concealing your love.
The hardest part is not waiting for them to love you back.
No.
The hardest part?
Waiting for something that may never happen
and watching the person who makes you happy,
be happy in someone else's arms.

Morgan Ashley Thomas
Saint Charles, MO

I am a senior at St. Charles High School. Originally, I started writing to get stuff off my chest or relieve stress. Everything I wrote I kept to myself until I took creative writing. Since then I started writing poems about anything that pops into my head. My inspiration is always a situation that either someone close to me or myself has experienced.

Heavens Meet the Mountains

One and true, I flew
By light of day and dark of night
To where the ground beneath my feet
Would kiss the skies.

And, awe! It dawned upon
This hollowed soul
That by way of true adoration
The skies would kiss back.

For when Heaven's doors agape
They expose the mountains and the seas,
And fallen angels descend
To their delight.

Yet man stands nervously
At the edge of the sky
With arms outreached, begging
For the stars to fall and carry him away.

Timothy Hunter Jack
Durango, CO

A Plea for Love

My lips are thick
My nose is wide
My eyes are almost round
My hair is short and curly
My skin the color of brown

Not in the hearts of brotherly love
Does this make me less a man
God still loves me, as should you
Though my skin be a darker tan

My hand is outstretched
Is yours for me?
Shall we be friends, we two?
And live in peace and harmony
As God would have us do.

Elizabeth Crudden
Columbia, CT

I am a white sixty-two-year-old teacher raised in a diverse community. My childhood friendships with many African Americans inspired my poem. When visiting a relative in 1960, I noticed the bathrooms and water fountains were labeled for "whites" or "coloreds." The "coloreds" had to sit in the back of the bus. I asked my mother why? She said it was different here. I did not like it! I said at my school everyone uses the same bathrooms and water fountains. We sat where we wanted to on the bus. In 1965, I wrote this poem for a school writing assignment on love. Children are born "colored" blind. We need to love one another.

Untitled

There are numerous things
in life we can control
and a few that we cannot.
Most serious is death;
my life has changed a lot.

Love from many friends,
and a tender touch from God...
made the void easier to manage,
than it was at first.
But the loss of a child's love and respect,
only made it worse.

Perhaps someday,
the picture will be more clear...
when death of another parent comes into focus,
or is more near.

So please do more thinking
of the past and how things were,
Or don't, if you prefer...

Sing alone, play alone,
and no one will enjoy your music,
or the message it might confer.

Arlene P. Knapp
Fly Creek, NY

Knock… Knock

Seize the moment… do not hesitate
Opportunity comes, but will never wait

Move forward… do not delay
The moment that is here will fade away

If you neglect to fan the flame
Should the fire return, you are not the same

So respond with resolve; act with verve
Set your path… do not swerve

When the task is done and you attain a goal
Somehow you know you enlarged your soul

Addie Carol Hill
Edinburg, TX

My first and only poem to be published was written in December, 1941, shortly after Pearl Harbor. My high school newspaper published it, and my poetry writing began. The USA was at war all four years I was in high school, so life was real and earnest. After graduating from SMU, marriage, four children, several moves around Texas, and divorce, these experiences translated into many differences in people and places. Life is anything but dull or frivolous. I hope you enjoyed my poems. There are others.

Memories in Black and White

She picked up her high school annual
That lay there on the shelf,
Turned to an old photograph of her sweetheart
And herself.
Homecoming queen at the football game,
It was still a beautiful sight,
Moments frozen there in time
Memories in black and white
Turning through the pages, she came
Upon the part:
A phrase that said, "I love you,
I'll hold you always in my heart."
Then looking out across the way
She recalls like yesterday,
When he went overseas to fight
Doing what he thought was right.
Now sixty years have come and gone
And she still sets there all alone.
With her wrinkled skin and her silver hair
One can tell that she still cares.
For by her bed a candle burns
Still beckoning his safe return;
She'll hold him in her dreams tonight
And those memories in black and white.
Memories in black and white
Treasures stored forever,
Souvenirs that bring to life
Memories in black and white.

Charles Norman
Uvalde, TX

Life

Life how different it can be
All the special ways it is presented that we see
As the days come and go without delay
When suddenly an event happens to our surprise
And if one is caught off guard
It could leave life like a great sunrise
Sadness comes when life turns and shows something missing from life
Where patience, grace and God's understanding
Changed longing into love
As He takes away from strife
Great news comes as a premonition
A baby will come to love and show great admiration
Pray for a wrong to be put right
God answered with a call for a child to come
A child for all to love and hold tight
A child to see, sent by God from Heaven above
In all things pray to God to prove with his might
He will always put you on a cause that is right
That is a cause that has less strife
A cause that helps everyone in their life

Mabel F. Gillespie
Millersville, MD

Love Everlasting

How can we grasp love everlasting?
Is it lying among our hearts so dear?
No, only time can bring those wondrous feelings
Beyond minutes, hours, days, and years.

Spend those moments enjoying joy and laughter,
Spend those moments in solitude and tears,
Only together sharing life's mysteries
Can you endure what others may fear.

Picture yourself among the flowers and branches,
Enjoying the company of one you hold near.
The world will not wait for you to be closer,
Sunlight and moonlight will soon disappear.

Fleeting is life on this bountiful planet,
Nonchalantly gliding through its colored haze.
By holding tight to your love everlasting,
You can find peace in all of its ways.

Elizabeth Ann Gregg
Troy, IL

This poem is dedicated to my husband who was diagnosed with Parkinson's disease in 2013. He inspires me and is my love everlasting.

Nightmare Sonnet

As black streaks crossed my mind's eye,
From cloudy dreams and hollow empty cares,
Came a dark and hopeless, sad, starless sky,
And the clattering gambols of the night mares.
Peace finding no hope amongst their numerous hooves!
Passions and fears building with the thunderous roar!
Body and spirit reeling in search of sweet reproves.
Images filled with desperation, tumult and gore.
Corporeal feelings of being mired with the dead,
Pushing and kicking, struggling to break free!
Searching for a way home, a path back to my bed!
Fighting back from the bottom of a dark, endless sea!
Ascending through the surface with a gasp and a scream,
Soaking wet, out of breath thinking, oh! what a dream!

Poet W. R. Foss
Port St. Lucie, FL

No Air

"I can't breathe." The familiar sound
echoed from cigarette sellers on corners
from those waving fake guns
from those left in backseats of locked cars
and abandoned day care vans.
"I can't breathe." You hear it from
those looking for jobs
those looking for mental health facilities
those looking for honesty.
"I can't breathe." As déjà vu surrounds us
and memories of tear gas, and
hungry dogs and
burning buildings… engulf us.
Don't you see?
It won't matter
when the wells are dry and
when the soil is barren and
when the heat of the day consumes us.
It won't matter
if you're black or white or yellow or red
if you're rich or poor
if you have health insurance.
We'll all stand in our empty fields
and quiet neighborhoods, whispering what we
no longer have the strength to say aloud…
"I can't breathe."

Michelle Satchell
Stone Mountain, GA

Color of Honor

When we are little, we are taught
the color wheel is very pretty.
When we grow, we are taught,
the color wheel has a whole new meaning.

Pink comes with pain,
green is jealous, white is cane.
Red is hot, blue is cold,
purple calms, and black is bold.

Pink for me, means something new;
same with green and yellow,
as well as red and blue.
Pink for me means fight,
with strength and determination.
Pink means I will survive,
with no humiliation.

All the colors today,
come with a ribbon around it.
All come with honor,
as we all somehow will survive it.

Theresa Wehrle
North Adams, MA

Angel in the Night

An angel comes calling who was removed from his employ
Looking to steal the hearts of every girl and boy.
Give me your souls little darlings, let me in.
He pleads with a voice of silk soaked in the blood of men.

An angel comes calling from dark of night to light of day.
Our souls become entrapped by his songs when he sings;
Give me your hearts little darlings, let me in,
He says with a voice of velvet warped by sin.

Oh blessed be holy, Lord, please lead us through this night.
Untouched by sin, uncorrupted by evil, into the morning's light.
Let your will be done, with these lives to us you've given
So that we may count this night as a struggle to overcome and a triumph to exalt in.

Keva J. Judge
Furman, SC

Keva Judge is a native of South Carolina and a high school senior. She is a freelance writer and poet whose favorite poets are Edgar Allan Poe and Langston Hughes. When she is not writing, Keva is active with church and extracurricular activities. She is also an avid animal and science fiction lover. Keva feels very blessed to have a family that is very loving and supportive of her passion for writing.

Fire-Dancers

They dance and dance in the pale moonlight,
Glowing brightly by fire's light.
Their eyes aglow in the darkened sky,
The flame-dance has begun.

The fairy folk all come to see,
Them dance to the Nokken's song,
Prancing about till morning light,
The dancers have taken flight.

Hidden among the likes of man,
None ever dream to see,
The beauty of dancing folk,
That make the fairies sing.

They toil among the sons of man,
And gain a hard-earned wage,
But once a moon they come again,
To dance on the forest's stage.

The fires glow amongst the wood,
The night has just begun,
The Huldra peek from out the brush,
In hopes of seeing one.

They are the creatures with unknown name,
They live among mankind,
Yet 'tis the ones you'd never think,
That dance through the flaming night.

Arielle Marlin
Nashville, NC

10 Gifts from God

1 a baby's smile
2 a budding plant
3 a singing bird
4 a playful puppy
5 a loving touch
6 a stranger's smile
7 a job well done
8 a perfect pie
9 a parent's pride
10 a real good cry

Alice Yates
Pleasant Grove, AL

My name is Alice McCart Yates. Living these eighty-nine years has been an interesting journey. I am a mother of: five beautiful daughters (I lost one, but she's still with us), eight beautiful granddaughters, five handsome grandsons, fourteen lively grandkids, and one great-grandson. What do you think? God gave me this awesome family to love and guide. They return the love and joy constantly. There are many others who call me "Big Nanny." I am blessed.

The Conductor

A tribute to Coach Dean Smith

You were the conductor
Of a symphony orchestra
In motion
You and the players
Working in unison.
Each doing his part
With precision.
You wrote the music.
It was your decision.
Your signals and gestures
Were your baton.
You knew the full score,
And your players won.
Your offense was Pacabel's
Canon in D.
Your defense was Rimsky-
Korsakov's "Flight
Of the Bumblebee."
When your duty was done,
Two national championships
Were won.
Your performance
Was the mold
For winning UNC
Players' souls.

Jessie Epps
Whitmire, SC

The Love of God

The love of God came from Heaven above,
To show us the true meaning of love.
We Love Him because He first loved us,
And we should always show Him our trust.

When He shows us the love He has revealed,
He tells us all His love is real.
Love one another for love is of God.
He showed His love while on the earth He trod.

God says to love thy neighbor as thyself,
For it will mean more than all your wealth.
If you love God with all your heart,
He will always be with you and never depart.

How can you believe a God you cannot see?
Just look all around and you will believe.
If you don't believe God's love is true,
Just pick up the Bible and read it through.

Now is the time to show others our love.
It was given to us from God above.
Remember God's love is a gift, it's free,
Our ransom was paid in full when,
He sent His Son to die on Calvary.

Emily McCormick
Cumming, GA

Forever Lost in Your Heart

You had me from the beginning,
Now I don't see it ending.
You are the partner on my path,
And the bubbles to my bath.
Even if we are miles and miles apart,
I'll be forever lost in your heart.

I can't believe this is real,
When I see you, it gives me a thrill.
You are the paw to my cat,
And the ball to my bat.
Ever since the start,
I was forever lost in your heart.

I was once lost,
But my love paid the cost.
You are the window to my pane,
And the thunder to my rain.
I found my missing part,
Now I'm forever lost in your heart.

Madison Lea Rich
Waynesboro, TN

Cancer

Cancer
raise your ugly head

Take away the security
of my world as I knew it

Fill my thoughts with doubts
and this head with visions of my own death

Strip me to the bone
making me vulnerable
helpless
and pathetic even to my own eyes

Take away the eyes of pity
that confirm my deepest fears

Cancer
you ugly
beast

You can take all from me
but the love that fills my heart

And the reminder of the true love
that I will meet some day

I will fight you with every breath
I have left

I will not submit to your
every whim

I am strong
and my hate
for you is equally so

Keitha Sharp
Oskaloosa, IA

Christmas 2014

'Twas the month before Christmas, and all through the land,
No snow could be found, only fluffy white sand.
The wreaths were all hung, on the doors with care,
With hopes that friends and family, soon would be there.
And Nana with her golf clubs, and Papa with his too,
Had just settled in their golf cart, with plans to "play a few."
When out on the street, we heard someone call,
Welcome back "snowbirds," we've been waiting for y'all!
And what to our wondering eyes should appear,
Our "snowbird" friends we hold so dear.
More happy moments came, and I'll call them by name,
Now Brian, now Alicia, now Jacob and Gabe,
Now Taina and Doug.
Makes for a warm family reunion, a reason for a long waited hug.
The grandkids are nestled, in new schools this year,
As college and high school freshmen, they are both happy we hear.
And then in a twinkling, I heard someone say,
Better get busy... it is almost Christmas Day!
As I drew in my head and was turning around,
The "reason for the season" came with a bound!
He isn't dressed in fur, so the story goes,
What *He* is wearing, no one knows.
We know *He* is the reason we celebrate the day,
It is also the reason this greeting is coming your way.
And now laying my pen aside for the year,
We hope this greeting has brought you some cheer.

Phyllis Greseth
Kenyon, MN

Missing You!

Mama, your face is the last I see,
When I close my eyes each night.
And since you went away,
My world is not as bright.

You are the first to cross my mind,
When I crawl out of bed each day.
I love and miss you so much,
My life will never be okay.

I long to wrap my arms around you,
And hold you oh so tight.
Wish there was something I could have done,
To make everything alright.

No matter how much I wanted to keep you,
I could not prolong your stay.
Because God was calling your name,
When he sent his angels that day.

Time heals all wounds,
Is what most people seem to say,
But the pain within my heart,
Seems never to go away.

All the good times we shared,
Are embedded deep within my heart.
And all those loving memories,
I will never ever part!

Ernestine Watters
Colmesneil, TX

Angels' Eyes

Look at the world
Through
Angels'
Eyes
And
You
Will
See
Them
Everywhere

It is only with the
Heart that one can
See what is invisible
To the eyes

Kimberley Grace Perks
Brampton Ontario, ON

Not Dead

No longer a score to settle
It's done, finished
No more a boiling kettle
All has diminished
We know who won the bout
And fought to the very end
In my mind there is no doubt
You were all pretend
Real the torment
And unyielding the drain
But I went the full extent
And now continue my reign
Where you took sanctuary
May you find your desires
I am sure you have no planetary
In whatever transpires
You will remain forever dismissed
But your words were noted
I live as though you don't exist
Laughably that means you were promoted

Venus M. Connelly
Tioga, PA

Lovely Fair Maiden

The skies roar high with storms now brewing,
Froth of waves beating a hull ensuing.
Skipped like a stone upon a pond,
Water sizzles from the great beyond.

Ether bears down alights the deck,
A frail matron quivers, from toe to neck.
Tossed about she clutches aft corner,
An' dares to pray against the maris horrors.

From her lips shudders my name,
The torrent is greater drowns her voice tame.
Gusts of wind announce thy entrance,
From the dark hold appears my vengeance.

Her Savior holds his balance around mast,
As rain pelts across his pout aghast.
"Catherine! Catherine!" The earth swallows his cries,
"Come to me my love." The helm does fly.

From whence she was only ribbon from garment,
Her figure replaced, save only her torment.
The weather veils tears, oh hallowed screams,
Briny beast has engulfed, love of lady in schemes.

"Please dear God! I shan't live deprived sir!"
And so he leaps into the emerald that shrouds her.
A saga that ends in grim pun laden,
The name of the vessel "Lovely Fair Maiden."

Edward William Berger
Acworth, GA

Cruel Reverie

When you think that you're smart
Until she looks at you
And you see her staring through you
From head to shoe

When things she says cannot be said
And her thoughts, unlike yours,
Cannot be read

When the thought of desperation creeps into your mind
As a bead of perspiration seeps down your spine

For the thought of a mistake, a misstep, an unfortunate event
Becomes too much to bear, to hold
On the twisted back that holds up the soul

For you think, "One shot, this is it, it must"
And you race towards her, oozing with lust
The step, uncertain, but eventually true
It turns out, to your luck, she was thinking of you too

You go with it, the smooth ball is rolling
But in the distance you hear a bell tolling
The sound grows louder as things grow more dim
Then suddenly, the shrill repetition stops coming from within

You reach towards your right, the opposite of delight
As you say good-bye to that mystical dream of last night

Tucker Joseph Matus
Royersford, PA

Fault

Higher higher the eagle flies
Softer softer the soldiers cried
Hurray hurray the enemy died
Swiftly swiftly the towers fell
Defeat defeat our faces read
Fight fight our nation cried
War war the soldiers died
Vengeance vengeance the people cried
Justice justice will come in time
Peace peace Lady Liberty cries
End end we cannot find
Pleading pleading on our knees
Heavens heavens set us free
Save us save us from a nation of lies
Deceit deceit we follow blind
Free us free us our children will cry
Oh this world this world we leave behind
Downward downward the eagle flies
Softer softer the soldiers died
Hurray hurray the enemy cried
America America
We tried we failed...

Diamond Dezira Dawn Bogle
Bartlett, KS

I'm a country girl from Kansas. We are about as American as it can get. It makes me sick to think that our great country is slipping down a steep slope. I love this country and I'm so proud to be an American. That's partly what this poem is about. It's about the people just following blindly what government tells them is right. We should be thinking for ourselves and making this country whole again. I don't want the lines in this poem to come true, but I'm afraid it's inevitable!

Seasons of Change

Apple orchards, river walks, corn maze
The scenic drive along the river—
Gorgeous colors changing

Beautiful leaves flipping, carefree in the wind
Animals gather food, scurry about
Hayrides, picking pumpkins

As leaves fall from the trees,
The air fills with scent of crisp leaves
Autumn leads us to colder weather—darker days

Gail Ann Wilson
Osceola, IA

I am currently a student at Simpson College in Indianola, Iowa, majoring in accounting. The area of learning that has been the most difficult for me has been writing. I had an opportunity to take a poetry class to help face my fear of writing. My instructor introduced numerous forms of poetry and creative writing through a workshop setting. She had more confidence in my writing than I had in myself. The inspiration to write this autumn poem came from this class and my professor who taught me how to write about a wonderful experience in my life.

Miraculous Rebirth

A mucus covered embryo
coming from your flesh.
Cracking through the surface
my blood coated skin.
Bony fingers reach.
Struggling amidst the fight
pushing, grasping, clawing
my head out to regain sight.
As I do and knobby elbows
charley horse your side.
Silently your screams
of anguish turns to delight.
In the moment of attainment,
I have freed my slimy body,
to once again believe:
That nothing's ever holy.

Angela Driskell
Anderson, IN

Tempus

Bing.
Got to get up, go to school, and do my classwork.
Sit in front of infantile children,
who jab their feet into my chair.
Released after the final bell, rush home, do my homework.
Rinse, recycle, and repeat.
And yet, I can't help but wonder,
if I had more time,
I could comprehend the meaning of whispers of the books,
begging me to learn their stories.
To journey to the sparkling stars in the crisp winter sky,
and be back before morning.
To finally discover—bing.
Time's up.

Juliet Smith
Kingstowne, VA

Your Fight

I know how hard you were fighting to stay
You fought night and day
You didn't want to go
You wanted to stay and play
But you grew tired
Tired of fighting what was in you
Tired of fighting to stay just one more day
Tired of growing weaker
And just plain tired
You knew how sad I would be if you went
So you tried harder to stay
Just for me
But the day came anyway
Too tired to fight anymore, you gave in
I know you had to go
I just wish I could have said good-bye
Wait for me in the sky

Marsha Lynn Raub
Barstow, CA

A Thought

I'll get a little camper and in it hide my face.
I can't understand or maneuver in this given purifying place.
No pain no gain.
I run to get away,
Straight into another one that was way out of the way.
Why can I not submit!
And change my selfish being.
I know I've a helper inside,
So, up and take wing.

Mashon Gaddis Coleman
Trenton, GA

Having, teaching, exploring, training and keeping up with five children and a husband puts a lot of spokes on each other's wheels. One is always in need of truing to get the wobble out. Representing seven states—Illinois, Georgia, Idaho, North Carolina, Montana, Oregon and Alabama—we've experienced the beauties and blemishes of each one. Being on a home island for twenty years does not shelter you from life with all its senses. I may have missed out—yes, on mono-culture, fads, career, independence and buzz words, but not human emotion. My poem was just the few that I wrote down.

Candy

when you are companionless
what is it you contemplate
is it contented and composed
or crazed and cruel

coked or comatose
which character will I make you
cranked, cracked, and cheated
you can't combat me anymore

concede me the counteractive
of your complications and concerns
I will cohere to you like cement
chasing away the corrupt

obscured in the clutch of chaos
I'm your conclusion, your wrong choice
candy fixing calamity
a calm purgatory

Leala Rachelle Adams
Harts, WV

The Missing Girl

I woke up and made coffee
As I rolled a cigarette the thought crossed me
We were out of milk so it was going to cost me
A trip to the store for a gallon or more
I came to the aisle and I saw your smile
At first I smiled then it turned to denial
It was your face down the sides of the dairy aisle
The picture was of you but from years before
Before the hordes of this world twisted your soul
Into words still unformed
Your beautiful face just so out of place
On the back of a milk carton
Underneath your picture was a good-bye written
By your mother and father
They were begging and pleading and
Wrote what they were screaming
Never believing you would be leaving
Their love for you would never be fleeting
But as I looked closer I got confused
I was absolutely sure that this person was you
But when I looked at the date from when you went missing
It said it was ten years from now so I suggest that you listen
Live life for today for your family and for you
Follow your heart and your dreams that's all you can do
It's time you let go of all of your fears
Only then will your picture on the carton disappear

Alex T. Keith
Dover, NJ

This poem, to me, is about reflection: what we and what others see in ourselves. We've all made mistakes. All you can do is try to be a better person today than you were yesterday.

Crime

Life
It's so long I don't remember when it started
The suffering I feel has reached its limit
The canary's unsureness

Juliet Tun
Hemet, CA

I am Juliet Tun. I am part Carian. The poem is about bearded women who are Carian.

9-11-01

What happened to the god of grape?
Dionysus, Bacchus and all their frenzied dancers,
Elevated by the Christ
To a dance of hearts, even of spirit.
Transcending earthbound humanity,
Knowing the flow of loving joy.

But an older god has seized the stage
Definitely steeped in righteous rage
With long, hard props that penetrate
Through diaphanous steel and glass
He inseminates his spawn of flame
The heart-hating god of rape.

Kevin Haggerty
Greensboro, NC

Hieroglyphs

Barren habits
Borrowed in a winter thaw
Six days past to seven
Hunger there and here imagined
Thirst in desert greenery
Appetites never sated
In an epic wild
Twilight yearnings
And a tired hope

Can you be more
Than I have ever hoped
To dream to dare
And having heard and felt
A beat that pulsed
Without the loss
And warmth of ecstasy?

I might be sure of songs
Written without words...
Thoughts of electron light
Bending toward the future's present
Formed in the skeleton of past Januaries
Fallen trees marking bark brown
Hieroglyphs in white

Geoffrey Rockwell Boynton
Warwick, NY

Years ago, I got a degree in English and even went on to graduate school. Necessities yanked me in different directions and I spent most of my years building houses and pursuing real estate opportunities. On occasion I write, mainly to my wife, which pleases her. I have acquired a certain wisdom in this activity which also pleases me.

Where I'm From

I'm from the icy cold ice rink with stuffy smells of green grass
I'm from boats floating on the great Mississippi River
With the crazed Cardinal fans eating crisp Cracker Jacks
From St. Louis to Taiwan

I'm from the crave of soy sauce eggs and crispy Peking duck
Crunchy Chinese noodles and flavorful dumplings
I'm from soft creamy tea eggs
To oily fried noodles
I'm from the fishy smell of sushi
From tuna rolls, salmon rolls, and fish eggs
I'm from salt grilled salmon and juicy pork chops
I'm from zip lines to paintball, candy guns and big swings
I'm from beads flying while watching the marvelous Mardi Gras parade
To the colorful fireworks of the 4th

I am filled with crazy cats and kittens
I am my favorite cat Adie who is as soft as a cloud
I'm from the loud motorcycles and buzzing supermarkets
I'm from tasty food in the street markets
I am from Taipei 101 and crispy chicken
I'm from the pink sparkly ice skating dresses that shine like a star
To big trophies and shiny medals
I am a creative, passionate, determined, ice skating, cat loving girl

Elizabeth Wangley
Creve Coeur, MO

Eclipso

I wonder if you are able to see me
Through the haze of smoke and rehabilitation
Or am I like the smoke rings
That fade away into the dark?

Cough a little louder
A point where you are scared to death
And we sold everything for this place
Even our hearts and souls

Eclipso
Your eyes are darkening and the sun
Shines a small ray through the closed blinds
You are just a shadow

Eclipso
Mi amor
Tu eres un monstruo
Mi amor

You rise with the smoke rings and the sun
And fall into the black horizon

Eclipso

Te amaré hasta que tu vuelvas de la oscuridad

Dominique Lydia Coleman
San Antonio, TX

Dominique Coleman is a North East School of the Arts creative writing and cinema major. She has always had a passion for writing and film. "Eclipso" was inspired by her father's, Billy Cano's, favorite song and is dedicated to him. He has been her mentor, friend and guardian in a life which has crafted her into the writer she is today. Lastly, she believes that words are inevitable. Writing is inevitable. Writers are lives dedicated to living millions of lives in the span of one lifetime. So grab a pen and go.

Dream

The time is past
That time is gone
Reality:
Strikes down deep

It's right in the face
Don't like the taste
Belief:
It's not going away

Never meant to measure
Or resent the pleasure
Too blind:
You cannot see

What's looking back
Is a future that
Won't lead the same path's
"Dream"

Travis Shane Cobb
Saint Hedwig, TX

Sailing

When it rains
It really seems to pour,
That could never be more true

It seems as if
Every raindrop
Makes an ocean

And I've never
Been good
At sailing in stormy waters

Anna Ruth Hill
Sylva, NC

Stay in School

School is cool, have perfect attendance.
It's the rule.
I sit at my desk and do my best on a test.
I use a tool that is my brain to take in knowledge and go to college.
I don't complain, it is the rule.
Be on time for school, it's cool.
Do not go swim in a pool and do not be a fool.
Go to school. It is fun.

Coy Denton
DeLand, FL

Pluto

The corners turn upward,
filled with cobwebs,
old books,
and dust—
an unremarkable incident led
to the greatest turnover in the history of the past.
And the structure rips and tears,
despite careful movements.
Anything left untouched is fragile.
Inner beauty exposed.

Britany Kahle
Concord, NC

Britany Kahle is a poetess, wordsmith, and creative entrepreneur, whose goal in life is to help others find their soul within. Residing in North Carolina, she loves to hike and climb summits. Her collection of poetry, entitled Vade Mecum: An Adoxography, *revolves around lunar themes, which is where her poem "Pluto" comes from. Considered to be abstract poetry, Britany's work is meant to be open for interpretation. She plans on publishing soon. Other poetry and prose written by Britany can be found at www.britanyjk.blogspot.com.*

Mistakes

He made the same mistake…
Correction, mistakes

He trusted those that were strangers
Strangers? He thought they were friends

He left his loving family…
Family they once were

He is me
Don't end up like me!

Jesse Ray
Katy, TX

Time Stands Still

A quiet day sneaks behind you as the world is but the same.
The predictions to your beginning were nothing but a slow decay.
Seeking for a sense of purpose,
we confine ourselves in such a relative time,
but this is only for the end of a mechanical function.
A glimpse of a kind-hearted soul lit up the tired room.
The spark of life set in the people around as the fly.
The infinite sky stretched a little further to those
who could not remember the meaning of life.

Tiffany Marie Von Tungeln
Madison, AL

Time

My mind is an empty space field, nothing matters
No one can hear what I have done in the field
Just my bemusements and wonders
Of time and why it is so unkind
And so generous all at once
It takes my years, months, days and minutes away
While trying to give countless
Memories, lessons, and experiences
It scars me and heals me all at once
It shows me what my life was, is, will be, could be, should be
And won't be
It is ever mocking
Mocking my feeble attempts to stay a step ahead of its plan
Only to fail and stumble and learn to know better
Than to be a step ahead of the ever changing current that is time
It is the ultimate trickster
It has the people around you show you
What your life should be and lets you believe,
Believe that you have control over what you will be
It is the wisest being in the cosmos, or so it thought
I thought I could outrun time's grasp
And I ran, to a field, my field,
But little did time know that
In my field I am time and time is none the wiser
I get my timely, beaming existence
And time gets what it truly deserves

Joceline Emmelin Perez Rios
Indio, CA

Priceless

How patiently she sits, awaiting the steady hand
and the cold feel of paint from hardened bristles
to make her something beautiful.
It has been days since she saw her friends get bathed
in glimmering hues of poppy yellow and sapphire red,
but she knows it will soon be her turn to display
the sights locked in her artist's head.
Patiently, calmly, she rests on her easel,
blank and fresh as a new beginning,
in the hope that inspiration has not abandoned
the hand that holds the brush
or the mind that holds the creation.
Perhaps, when the time comes, she'll taste a melancholy design,
one bathed in dark blues and midnight secrets.
Or maybe she'll be covered in the brightest of colors,
ones that make her feel warm and loved beneath her cotton skin.
But to her, it doesn't matter what people will see
when she is freshly designed,
still shining like the slick coat of a brand new baby calf.
To her, she will always be a masterpiece worth displaying.
And that is what makes her priceless.

Stephanie Gerlach
Blanchester, OH

Meet You All Over Again

If I could meet you all over again,
I wouldn't be afraid of the butterflies.
I'd cover my scars,
Force the edges of my lips to curve
And let you wrap your body around me.

If I knew how much I'd love you,
I would memorize the lines around your eyes
Every time you laughed at our jokes
So I could always remember how happy we once were.

If I knew how much it would hurt without you,
I'd fall in love with you sooner.
We'd spend more Sundays at home
And less birthdays apart
Just so the memories could fill your place in bed.

Distance and time can mend what we broke
And our tears will eventually subside.
I'll wait for your hand on my cheek,
A kiss on my head,
And the chance to meet all over again…

Iris Michelle Delgado
Washington, DC

I was raised by strong women in New Jersey who came to this country wanting a better life for their children and family. I write for them, for the words they were afraid to say and emotions they may have never admitted to feeling. I was inspired by their love, great food and warm hugs and by the man who has taught me the meaning of love.

A Girl's Best Friend

Roses are red, violets are blue,
I don't know what I'm going to do with you.

You might be smelly, you might be nice
I don't care as long as you are mine.

You make my heart go boom so loud,
You're like a diamond in a huge crowd.

You're so great you break my heart,
To be honest it might break apart.

You're the one I treasure the most,
What a pleasure I have a friend like you!

You're the one who will be my friend til the end of our friendship!
The end.

Camdyn Leigh Vermillion
Hays, KS

The Blues

Calling, texting, maybe a tweet,
That's what we do to get friends on their feet.
Go to the movies, share a laugh,
Doesn't matter how much time has passed.

Walking, talking, maybe a smile,
Take their thoughts away for a while.
Dinner, dishes, that's what we do,
To help a friend get out of the *blues*,

So pick up that phone and be that friend,
Who no matter what will be there in the end.
Don't be afraid to show your face,
'Cause we don't know what it's like to be in their place.

Mark Braithwaite
Clinton Township, MI

I started writing poems after my father's death in September of 2013. I am married with two boys, ages seventeen and fourteen. My oldest son was diagnosed with a tumor and I was looking up poems to cheer him up. I stumbled across a contest on how to cheer up a friend and wrote my poem, "The Blues," in less than fifteen minutes. Once I started writing it I could not stop. I myself am a finish carpenter who works for a union company. We are currently helping to rebuild Detroit.

Sweeter Love

Alone for days and nights
As work for him is urgent
Always busy.
I seem to see him always
Passing by
The steady rise and fall of his back
As he sleeps beside me.
Alone still in our togetherness.
My daily mantra breathing,
In and out.
In and out.
Motivated by the steady hum of
Chores and children.
And I pray to merciful God
For a sweeter love
Or a quicker death.

Toni Lynn Poling
Findlay, OH

Isabel

You were once so like the lilies you held,
Stunning. Delicately beautiful,
Never fragile in the free-flowing wind,
In which you would sway and bend.

But as you lay,
Chest cavity hollow in its still moving form,
Thorns clinging to the shirt-skins of angels,
Flowers drizzled in the dust of defeat.

Cracked tombstones of clear porcelain,
Blue-blood veins run dry under
Fragmented tiles.

The sun through skin blush
That once tinted cheek flesh,
Left alone the barren landscape,
With lack of rose bloom.

Gabriela Isabel Fortes-Jordan
Cary, NC

Brick and Mortar

Crimson brick building wall,
you watch the city scream
before it lies awake in distant dream,
going in and out of hazy words from a faraway phone call.

Strung-together plastic coated wire,
you illuminate bulbs that brighten the city,
more rather the window that gazes out in pity
onto a world that ignores your efforts due to its ongoing fire.

Grungy streets of slick pavement,
you bear the burden of the busy day
from taxi tires and the puddles that spray
the not-so-white crosswalk tiles worn down to fragments.

Back to you, crimson brick building wall,
with mortar sealed in between your edges and aisles
of an exhausted exterior which designs your faded worldly style,
you are the epitome of existing, surviving, straight and tall.

Emily Stoddard
Riverview, NB

Pain

What is that feeling inside me, is it me feeling betrayed,
or hurt?
The feeling is unbearable that it makes me want
to go to a corner and cry, but that will make me weak
which I'm not.
I'm In control of my life and I will not have it taken from me.
But what if I can't bear the words I hear,
what if it brings me down even more than what is known?
Once you have that feeling it never goes away,
because once it starts it never stops,
but the words I may say they aren't true they
are false.
I am not strong I am very weak when it comes to this
feeling.
It hurts so much. Once I did not feel this pain I am now.
I was happy, I was joyful and I didn't care what happened
to my life, it was perfect, and nothing could go wrong.
But that has all now changed the pain is even worse the
words have came true now I'm stuck in this forever.
And my pain will go on, I may not be fine I will be invisible
to what I know now and may forever.

Sierra Irene Torres-Hutchison
Coshocton, OH

2015

Back to the Future, Doc and Marty
"On the Road Again," Paradise and Moriarty
Predictions can be made so complex
When "dealing" with Dio's like Dr. X

A Miami "Marlins" baseball team
Lion's playing on a beach—Santiago's dream
They tell you, "Inherit the Wind"
But, you are obsessed with, "Original Sin"

Trickster, con man, saint?
What we need is a portrait of Pocahontas paint
"When 'The Game' Stands Tall"
Will "Africa" rain, as "Stanley Falls?"

Spaceballs, lyrics of Stephen Schwartz
The mayor's son, perhaps he will see the police "force"
Pull out his eyes/apologize?
"When You Believe," you see, "Through Heaven's Eyes"

Follow, "The Napoleon of Crime?"—no "small" feat
Like Shelley's, "Ode to the West Wind," he had a "Beat"
And if you're asked, "Is Sting the 'King of Pain?'"
Refrain? "The Man with no Name"
Is a drifter of a higher plain

Paul Szymanski
Patchogue, NY

The "monomyth?" or your own "personal legend." My life was influenced by my parents, Stanley Szymanski and Barbara (nee) Nugent. Like Paulo Coelho, the writer of The Alchemist, *I was misunderstood, but still loved. Joseph Conrad's,* Heart of Darkness *and* Secret Sharer, *were my life "force." Poetry became an outlet. I often speak about Jesus. However,* The Poisonwood Bible, *by Barbara Kingsolver, forces me to think about the police in my own country and "seeing" the different perspectives on religion, race, law, and nature throughout history. See* Springtime for Hitler—*LOL.*

Untitled

it's like a gash that can't be stitched.
my best friend, you were my best friend.
the pain, so unbearable.
the memories, they're so good.
the hurt it brings me to look at your face.
the tears, so many fall on your picture.
come back.
this life, the laughs, aren't the same.
our bond was unbreakable, my best friend.
the hurt, God it hurts.
my angel, my sweet angel.
the thought of seeing you again, brings me joy and a smile that will not fade.
if I knew that the last time I saw you, was the last time, I would have never taken my eyes off you.
it feels so unreal, the reality, that I cannot face.
the numbness.
as I sit and stare, at nothing.
my heart sinks so far down.
my angel, watch over me.
watch me grow, and live.
be there for big times, like my wedding.
when I'm dancing, you'll be dancing with me in my heart, my best friend.
watch me make everyday count as I make my way up to you.
feel joy, angel.
my heart has been broken by the thought, the thought of you not being here.
but it heals a little bit more everyday, knowing someday, we will reunite.
fly high my sweet angel, fly so high.

Chaney Crum
St. Francisville, LA

The Loving Tree

Because our ten-day courtship was coming to an end,
We needed a living symbol to allow our romance to grow.
After walking the rows of evergreens and shrubs,
We spotted our "Loving Tree" at the local nursery,
For only Ann and me to see.

It was early morning when I walked out to see,
That "Loving Tree" before I planned to leave.
I wrote a note upon a card and placed it in the pot,
For only Ann to see.

The note was short and sweet!
It said, "Dear Ann,
    My true soul mate... keep it alive while I'm gone!
    Always loving you... our Loving Tree,
For only Ann and me to see.

And now my friends, with school bells in the air,
I have returned to see that "Loving Tree."
And what a tree to see... Her loving care to share,
That "Loving Tree" for only Ann to see.
And for me to be,
The proud owners of that "Loving Tree."

Dennis L. Johnson
West Palm Beach, FL

The Plea

Pow! Pow! go the guns of those in the street.
Is violence to others the answer?
The death of those from guns in the street
and mothers sit home and are weeping.

Pow! Pow! go the guns on the battlefield.
Is violence to others the answer?
The death of those on the battlefield
and mothers sit home and are weeping.

Are weapons the answer to war in the street?
Are bombs the answer to war?
Mothers speak out, don't sit at home.
Work for peace instead of weeping.

Teach love and respect to your sons and daughters.
Teach dialogue instead of the shooting.
Guide the world to change and take up the cross.
Then mothers someday can stop weeping.

Suzanne E. Grade
St. Louis, MO

Needless to say, I was inspired by events in our world and events in and around the area I live in. I'm a retired teacher, married mother of two, grandmother of three, and yes, I did teach creative writing for a while. I was a recipient of the Thanks to Teachers Award from Apple Computers, twice on Outstanding Teacher of America, a recipient of a writing award from the St. Louis Post-Dispatch, *a recipient of an award using aviation in education, a Distinguished Alumni of Harris Teachers College awardee, a finalist from* Weekly Reader *in the Use the News contest, and awarded several blue ribbons for class projects in area science fair.*

Common Ground

There's common ground though we may not be alike
May really be different as day and night.

Those who have it all will seek for simple pleasures
Those with little consider simplicity their treasure.

When we've had things we've wanted
Collected our dolls and trinkets
As we grow older and look at our stuff
Having time to rediscover and to rethink it.

What gives the heart peace and a sense of ease
As we play, giggle, and tease?

The pleasure of sitting, watching a sunrise
Beauty of faces and the color of skies.

As you move from day to day, no matter where your place
Enjoying the privilege of a new day to face

The human spirit has a common ground
In each person, this is surely found.

The Spirit has no color, no religion, no codes to direct or
connect and no particular season.

We're moved by it, lifted by it
It can always fit
As we keep on our journey, never to quit.

And here are words I read
And I would like to share:

As Rumi said—

"Beyond the idea of right doing and
wrong doing—there is a field—

I'll meet you there."

Sherry A. York
Arab, AL

A Mother's Love

My dear sweet daughter!
I love you so,
You've brought me more love and joy,
Than you'll ever know.

You're only a baby,
So sweet and so kind,
You're such a sweet child,
I'm so blessed that you're mine.

To all you mothers,
I think you'd agree,
To have your own daughter,
Is as sweet as can be.

You will love her forever,
You will protect her each day,
You will cry at her wedding,
On her special day.

Robin Hellman
Trenton, FL

Sin

My mind is entrapped by your sinister smile
Your poison on drip, I am in denial
Running from you is impossible, you won't let me leave
Why must you make me sit here and believe?
Believe that when I listen to you I feel great
When in reality all I feel is hate
You consume me, tearing me apart limb by limb
Letting me suffer as you grin
I try to fight you but you always win
They can't see it with their eyes or read it on a page
But soon your terror they will have to face
Why must you have no compassion or will?
Instead all you want to do is steal
Steal my heart right out of my chest
I become another person with you I'm possessed
While you steer the real me with shackles
And beat me to death
Death now in my eyes like no one is left…

Christine Oberkirch
Daphne, AL

I've always been mesmerized by the way poetry can illustrate the beauty and complexity of one's mind, the fact that words on a piece of paper can unlock trapped emotions. I wanted to make that impact. I wanted to write poems that widened people's view on life around us. I started writing after my first trip to the hospital. I was drowning and no one was around to hear me scream. So I wrote and all the emotions flew out enabling me to breathe. It was then I fell in love with writing, and I let it become my life.

Facebook

Facebook's a form of communication
With friends both here and there.
They can communicate anytime
And keep in touch anywhere.

They can share their friends with others
Who, in turn, become friends.
The list continues to keep on growing
With each one adding new friends.

This reminds us of Jesus Christ,
Our Lord, our Savior, our friend.
When we tell others about God's Son,
And they accept Him as their friend.

One way in which this greatly differs
From the Facebook list of friends:
People can be "unfriended" on Facebook
If they're no longer wanted as friends.

How humiliating to be "unfriended,"
As they see it there in print,
And learn that their friendship has been rejected
Without being given a hint.

One thing that they can always count on:
From His list, God will never "unfriend"!
Unless they continue rejecting His Son,
On His "friends" list, they'll stay without end.

Joyce Folsom Johnson
Shapleigh, ME

My Favorite Hobbies

Buckets, bases, and bucks for this boy
I chase them all like a dog with his toy
After the national anthem, I hear, "Let's play ball"
When I hit the baseball it screams to the outfield
As I run the bases it sounds as if I were a galloping horse
After getting a base hit I know I've done my job
It makes me mad when the umpire calls a ball a strike
When I dive for a ball, I think to myself, don't miss it
I wake up early and go sit in the cold, peaceful woods
Sometimes I see a doe but I hope to see a buck behind her
Sitting in a tree stand can get boring
But seeing a deer always makes for an exciting hunt
When I aim at a deer I know I will feel the recoil from the shot
Nothing makes me madder than to hear a squirrel and think
it's a deer
When I'm watching a hunting show, I wish to kill a trophy
buck someday
I drip sweat as I dribble down the court for a perfect shot
I like hearing the swish when the ball goes in the net
Draining a three pointer to take the lead will always make me happy
I was happy when we won the basketball championship last year
Sometimes we win and sometimes we lose but I still have fun
Baseball, basketball, and hunting are my favorite hobbies
I hope to do them as long as I live

Nick Barker
Clover, SC

Alzheimer's Disease: We Must Find a Cure

Memory loss was common
And could not be controlled
Blamed on the aging process
As part of growing old
But then in 1906
A neuropathologist
Found why loss of memory
For years had been dismissed
Alois Alzheimer proved
All brain cells are attached
But with the slightest movement
These cells can be detached
There are billions of these cells
Linked together like a chain
That form part of a network
Wound together in the brain
There are no physical symptoms
So the body feels no pain
But memory will lessen
As cells die within the brain
But if these cells could be replaced
The body surely would
But since that's not possible
The news cannot be good

Stan Drescher
Flagler Beach, FL

I was born on New York's Lower East Side in 1931, one of eleven children. I started writing when in college at age sixty-five. Since then, I've written over one hundred poems and over twenty short stories. My themes cover illness, non-profit organizations, and Flagler Beach. I was inspired to write "Alzheimer's Disease: We Must Find a Cure" when a speaker at one of my clubs presented a program, gave out brochures, and asked for a donation. He was a motivational speaker and I felt the passion to commit his words to poetry. I'm the Poet Laureate of Flagler Beach.

The American Dream

Extremely generous this country has always been
Plenty of opportunities to further studies and work
America has distinguished among all others indeed
Meeting your expectations without sorrow or regret

Your citizen's rights are guaranteed
Your dreams always come true and your life is full of love
Your goals are well respected, your sacrifices as well
Enjoying a happy life, because it is well-deserved

Life may be easy for you by not wasting any time
Always trying your best to be the best among your life
It protects you, it lodges you and responds to all your needs
If you try really hard when doing things a masterpiece

Around the world America set the sample
Regardless of what others say
Protecting you from injustice, abuses and hearsay
Treat people as human beings with sincerity and good heart
Specially to the needy that always they have the right

Everybody around the world would like
To enjoy the American dream at large
But it is not easy to obtain unless you sacrifice yourself
Giving a hand to the needy without prejudice and dislike
Acting in very good faith and pray to the Lord
From the bottom of your heart and full of pride

Raimundo Matos
Spring Hill, FL

I am a retired Army veteran, with certain disabilities, after serving thirty-eight consecutive years. My first eleven years of service was in the regular Army and another twenty-seven years were with a state National Guard as a full time federal civil service employee. I have no formal musical or literary training, but I often write songs and poems. At present I have registered with copyright 161 poems and 125 songs, both in English and Spanish, all dormant and unedited in my personal library. What inspired me? Our God, Mother Nature and all human beings.

Wherever You Are

An exquisite smile as dazzling as the sparkle of a diamond.
Intense brown eyes which stir the yearning in my soul.
To hold your hand in mine is sensuous.
The rush of love and the surge of desire waves through my body.
Your gentle laughter consumes me until I cannot breathe without
hurting.
The current that saves me infects me.
Wherever you are is where my heart belongs.
We flowed like a river conquering its current, meanders and rapids.
Our commitment envied by all. Can we sustain the gauntlet of
the falls?
Broken pieces along the banks; love fighting for life.
Love is still alive. I feel it in your tears, yet gasping for air.
My heart lies helpless upon the banks.
A ready meal for the vultures, which circle in the blue skies
above me.
I throw my voice into the winds,
"Dear God Let Her Breathe."
My prayer: A miracle, your love returns.
Wherever you are is where I belong....

Kim Duval
Chicago, IL

Dedicated to Tawnya.

Parting Company

Having so much fun,
Running, laughing, holding hands,
Lying in the sun.

Put your head on my shoulder.
Let's just take a nap,
As the stress just melts away.

You nudge me awake.
Sunset means it's time to leave.
Tears shed on my sleeve.

Purple wraith from days gone by,
Blowing in the wind,
Never to be seen again.

Broderick Joel Burton
Sherman Oaks, CA

Burn the Boats

Burn the boats we can't return
We'll die here or survive
Fire the ships we won't look behind us
The past is forever gone
Char the vessels we aren't going back
Our fortunes lie ahead
Rise up with courage
Fear has no hold
Steel your mind, steady your heart
We leap beyond the familiar
New places, a great adventure
No reservations, no doubts
Burn the boats we're moving on
Forward to the dawn
Fire the ships we're moving out
Contingency will be our end
Char the vessels, leave it all behind
Reinvention starts today
New beginnings, unknown endings
Burn the boats, seize the day

Caleb Rassi
Tremont, IL

Dedicated to Taylor: without a doubt the best friend I've ever had.

Moonshine Visions

My courtyard Buddha
looks right at me,
sipping my latest moonshine.

My moonshine days
are filled with waterfall rays,
looking within and out again.

My mind,
once enlightened,
sees everything.

These moonshine days
have earned a special place
in my courtyard.

Heretofore, I shared only with Buddha,
my favorite mug of fiery brew that
fuels imagination.

Until now. Dear reader,
consider this your
invitation to join me.

Marc Livanos
Pace, FL

Magical Night

Magic is everywhere I can feel it in the air.
I see the fairies dancing there
so free and without care.
I join in their merry game,
and my life will never be the same.
We dance under the pale starlight,
as we fly throughout the night.
Night has now turned into day,
it's time for my friends to go away,
but I will see them when the moon is high
and magic fills the midnight sky.

Kayla Garraway
Mobile, AL

Snowflation

All snowflakes are little creations
Each unique bits of fascinations
One by one, they hold revelations

Charles James Bailey
Morristown, NJ

Charles Bailey is an eleven-year-old boy from New Jersey. He has seen an abundance of snow over the past two winters. His poem is inspired by those climatic experiences and his emerging skill at speaking his mind.

Betty's Retirement

Woe is us! What will the employees at CPP do?
We will have no one to take our problems to.
Who will take care of our insurance, savings and
security, DPA, our paycheck and more?
When Betty retires and walks out GE's door.
For thirty-four years the employees and General Electric
have really been blessed,
to have an employee who excelled at every
thing and always did her best.
It wasn't just the company Betty kept in mind,
she gave her co-workers a lot of her time.
There are no words to express how much
you will be missed,
having you as a co-worker and good friend
has been pure bliss.
Thank you for caring for us all the years;
you may have to excuse us as you
retire and we shed a few tears.
It is a real joy to honor you on this
your retirement day,
we do have one regret—that you can
leave and we must stay.
We hope happiness, good health, and prosperity
fill your retirement days,
may God bless you and keep you in His
care always.

Evelyn Dawson
Goldsboro, NC

My brother and I arrived at Baptist's Children's Home in Thomasville, NC, in August 1942, after the death of our parents. We were so blessed to have this as our home. I remained there until I graduated from high school in 1953. We return in August each year for homecoming. I moved to Goldsboro, NC, after graduation. I was hired by GE as an inspector. I worked for GE for thirty-six years, until I retired. In 1954, I married Nathan. We celebrated our sixtieth wedding anniversary on June 4, 2014. This poem I wrote for Betty when she retired from GE. I wrote more poems for our co-workers as they retired. They each received a framed copy of their poem at their retirement party.

A Girl Like Me

When you look at me,
What do you see?
A slim black girl, single parent,
Yes that's me.
But look deeper,
Deeper into my soul.
A transformation of
God is what you will behold!
His grace, mercy, and all the above
My God, my God
See the presence of His love!

Tomeko Brown
Raleigh, NC

Sometimes the world puts limitations on what we can become but no matter what the world thinks we are all individually handcrafted by God into a unique masterpiece. I grew up in a single parent household, the oldest of three. My mom always encouraged us to become whatever we wanted, but to just give it your all in whatever you do. She instilled faith, courage, and determination in all three of us. Today I instill those same attributes into my son and daughter.

Where Are the Children

A peaceful morning at a schoolroom lair
Interrupted by sound that filled the air
A tragedy played out in an innocent place
Comfort and safety left there to waste

This longtime haven where learning was sought
Disrupted by gunfire that a madman brought
Parents left shattered with lifelong pain
Struggling with sanity seeking who is to blame

What form of being determines why
These angels of the earth were chosen to die
Is there really a reason why lives had to end
Questions unanswered will forever transcend

Memories seem unnatural as we recall the pain
Why life was to be taken in a world so called sane
A shock that seeks purpose we continue to relive
Understanding what was lost was too much to give

Now we seem to struggle with gun control cause
Justifying automatic weapons without pain or pause
Lobbying meets politics with a posturing tact
Yet the outcome will never bring the children back

Thomas J. McNichol
Fort Mill, SC

Homage to the Sun

If, each day, I could
envision the sun's rays,
nay, not envision but *see*,
actually be in the midst of,
Rah!

For the sun ever-lasts,
indeed, it warmeth the heart,
warmeth the bones and
warmeth the very thought of ourselves.

Stand. Stand here under the golden rays,
the light which gives us
the strength we need to carry on.

Splendid, ye be splendid,
and I glory in the thought of that.

Rah, Rah, glory be to God
in the highest, for thee, oh sun,
the highest of the realm.

Is this ode over?
Shall this adoration suffice?

Praise the light,
praise the illumination
every day, as the dawn approacheth.

Beverly Whitehead
DeFuniak Springs, FL

Beverly Whitehead graduated from the University of Arizona where she was a research assistant in the folklore department of the English graduate school. Subsequently, she printed etchings and drawings for artist Ted de Grazia, depicting Indian children dancing under a warm Tucson sun. Was this the inspiration for "Homage to the Sun"? Partly. But simply living in the Southwestern desert was the major influence. I am now retired and enjoying family life.

Morning Sun

I woke this morning from a good night's sleep. I raised the blinds to take a peek. The sun was bright and not a cloud in the sky, it felt great just to be alive; at my age I never ask why.

I think so often of the days, months and years that have gone by so terribly fast, I stop at times and wonder what life is all about. I remember the past so very well. There are memories, laughter and tears as well.

So when I get up each morning, and peer out that window, I give thanks to God for the gift of life and for the memories I can share and for the many smiles I have left on the people who care. It marks the beginning of the day with many more smiles to come, friends to be made, and thanks to be given.

Well O Lord, thanks again for allowing me to enjoy that good night's sleep and to lift those blinds and peek at the sun. Thanks for yesterday. It was fun! But I promise that when you call, I'll be ready, no regrets, I'll be standing tall.

So, dear loved ones and friends, when you open those blinds in the morning and look at the sun and at the same clouds in the sky, look hard; it's me, it's me saying, "Good-bye."

William Broestler
Port St. Lucie, FL

I wrote this poem as I was recovering from neck cancer. Doctors gave me little chance of recovery. I found the days very long, as I fought this deadly disease, and the nights dark and dreary. I waited anxiously for morning and would go to the window for the morning sun. It felt great just to be alive, knowing I had to fight for another day. My poem unfolded as I lived it. So my friends, always look for that sun whenever it might appear. There is enough for all of us (you'll see). I am still here.

My Treasured Years

Where have the years gone, since I'm aging day by day?
In my mind I feel young, but in truth it's not that way.
I look in the mirror and what do I see?
I see a woman who looks like my mother, not me.

The wrinkles on my face, the circles under my eyes,
Adorn the face of an older me and do not tell lies.
When I was young, I'd daydream; such plans I had.
Days became weeks, some were good, and some bad.

As the weeks became months, goals were put on hold.
After becoming wife and mother, I wasn't as bold.
Resuming a career seemed daunting at first.
But testing my skills was for better, not worse.

Far better than staying at home and not knowing,
Was to test my wings and prove my worth by showing.
So I worked in an office and also cared for my family,
Until our children were grown and my husband needed me.

The months became years and the years took their toll.
My husband's health declined and suddenly we were old.
Now I'm alone with my treasured memories still clear.
The days, weeks and months are the years I hold dear.

Eleanor Egan
Johns Creek, GA

Susie Short

Miss Susie Short, born in May,
Led a *short* life in ev'ry way.

Tho' *short*-changed at birth (not a mere rumor),
Susie, in fact, had a good sense of humor.

Her daily antics, well-known and various,
Held no *short*age of actions hilarious:

She lengthened her chin and *short*ened her nose;
Just how she did it, nobody knows.

Still, temper in childhood was *short,* that is true;
And she did have a *short* attention span, too.

Susie, grown up, felt small and much slighted,
With both eyes weak and very *short*sighted!

Short in stature, Susie dressed sort of funny;
Well, wouldn't you, if you lived *short* of money?

A lot *short,* too, in little grey cells,
Susie Short managed to dodge wedding bells.

Instead, she kept slaving, as life demanded,
In dull, thankless jobs, forever *short*-handed.

At thirty she died, still making news,
Having *short*ness of breath—wearing stiletto, red shoes.

Lucy Worthen
Duluth, GA

I'm a 5' 1" native Atlantan. At age eighty-seven, I still whine about not being stately. Unlike Susie's short "faults," I'm short-waisted. What a bummer! Many years prior to retiring from the US Foreign Service overseas as a secretary, I served as secretary to the warden of Atlanta's US penitentiary. I had a lot to learn and did, in the FBI steno pool and, later, as a secretary in the US Secret Service. World travel (to fifty countries) in all those years was my delight. I relax now by continuing to read, write and listen to classical music. Here's to poetry proliferation!

The Seasons of Life

Springtime is here everyone is cheerful, all is well.
Then the summertime comes and lives start to fail.
Life was once carefree and full of cheer,
Now summertime has come, time has passed and joy has turned to fear.
Fall oh when it decides to come, now a river flowing with tears has just begun.
Tears are flowing like a river for the fall has taken our spring,
And with it so many people that once were among the living.
The seasons of life, they come and they go, so cherish each moment,
For when the dead of winter comes no one knows.

Wendy Warren Melvin Warliven
Clinton, NC

Heavenly Things

Summer, winter, fall or spring like the
Morning stars that sing,
Too the heavenly clouds it brings.

To see the beautiful horizon, that appears
Just across the eastern bay, we pray.

Oh! How lovely everything seems, in a
Very special way, that's heaven to me.

To see the clouds, filled with precious sights,
That makes special colors with rainbow delights.

To the highest mountains of many delights, that
Make heavenly moments, above many wingless flights.

To hear sweet melodies, from the beauty of birds
That sing to the trees, from the bees that bring
The honey, that's heaven to me.

There's untold joy, to reach the sky, that's deep from
The winds that blow, to the flowers that grow
To form beautiful bows, that's heaven to me.
To see the clear blue skies up high, God has given
Heaven to me.

Gevene Dobson
Miami, FL

Future of Tomorrow

Tell me, what this is all about? I wonder who is with me?
Will I become broken, amidst this unbroken world? Yet I
laugh, blinded to everything.
Being as uncertain as I am, I hold my breath, so my life
can be unraveled in this far off future.
Wonder what my life would be if time freezes. I try
finding you in this unshaken, twisted future. I gradually become
transparent, unable to be seen. I really don't want to hurt
anyone in this world. I can only imagine. What my life
would be if time freezes. In this far off unraveled future. So
please remember me, memories of times we laughed.
It seems gradually I become transparent. And I can't move,
this unraveling world tries to change me. Will I be able to go back
to the way I was?
In this unbreakable world I can't afford to be transparent.
Sometimes you try looking for me. If you cannot find me
will you give up? If I am trapped in solitude will someone else
try looking for me? As time passes by time seems to be unraveling
this bitter future.
You try to remember me, as best you can. But, it seems
that you have forgotten me. I am paralyzed by the fact that I
might lose you.
Will I know what paradise is, will I recover from being
transparent?
Please don't forget who I am. If you forget then I will
become transparent in this darkness.

John Lockwood
Winston-Salem, NC

Today, Tomorrow, a Lifetime

Tic tic tic, tock tock tock
We are the hands of the global clock

Our big blue marble spins around
We are to blame for poisoning our ground

Everyone get up it's not too late
Plant a tree, help clean up a lake

Take a walk, ride a bus, carpool or ride a bike
Sure these things may be things you dislike

Come on man!
Make a plan to preserve our land

Do it today for tomorrow may be too late
Cultivate, educate, bring ideas to your schoolmates

This world is in the palm of your hand
Pass it on, be the better man!

Colleen Beck
Lake Worth, FL

Alma Expuesta

Draped in black
Under the wisdom of silver hair
She dances her isolation

With impassioned eyes
Her fingers take flight
Ruffles and flourishes entwine
Above rumbling heels
Growing insistent

A voice of shadows
The bleeding guitarra
Palmistas anchor the pulse

Fiery, fluttering tangles
Ripple from her center
Seeking the duende
Infecting her blood

Lori Kullberg
Louisville, KY

Writing, for me, has always served as a tool of self-expression. What I could not say, I could write. Beginning some thirty-five years ago, I started penning my thoughts and it still gives me as much a sense of freedom as it did then. As the title of my poem translates, "Soul Exposed" is an expression of how I feel when I am dancing flamenco. It is passion, it is intensity, it is beauty, and it is me. Flamenco has touched a part of me I did not expect, providing endless surprises and joy.

Xenophilia

I reach out and savor
The caress of foreign objects
As they leave chalky memories
On the pads of my fingers.

Transitory feelings

That dance away with my breath.
Edges become soft,
Morphing into eternity
Etched in the hard planes
Of dying recollection.
Resurrection is unlikely:
Unnecessary

And so I forget their feeble grasp
When I regain my feet
And continue forward
Hoping to stumble again
And clutch at new memories…

Victoria Stone
Pittsburgh, PA

Birth and Death of a Newspaper

I started from a tiny seed, dropped by a jay in his time of need.
Warmed by the sun and fed by God, there I grew under the sod.
It took many years to become a big tree.
I stood tall and proud, through lightning and thunder and a big
rain cloud.
I housed many critters, like squirrels and their litters, an occasional
coon and a bear.
Then one day through the forest came men and machines on a tear.
Stripped of my branches, I lay naked and gray, sent off to the
mill so far away where I was stripped of my bark and chopped up
real small, and squeezed and soaked and rolled into a ball.
Until I was flat, all white and pretty. Printed with ink, then shipped
off to the city.
Thrown on a truck, folded and tied, I went for another bumpy ride.
Till I ended up by somebody's door, picked up by a dog and dropped
on the floor.
"First dibs on the sports," I heard a man say. A kid grabbed my
comics
and hurried away. "I'll take the locals," the sleepy wife pleaded.
It's nice to be wanted, fought over and needed.
Until I've been read up one page and down
And end up with the garbage outside of town!

Nancy J. Weiner
Avon, ME

Ginger

Ginger sits now in a wicker chair
Staring out the front window at the sunny day
Her clear blue eyes unblinking
Lashes beautiful and rosy cheeks
Her bright auburn hair pulled away from her face
With a cluster of curls falling down her back
What does she see?
Her quiet smile brightens up her face
Her pale blue organza dress
Is tucked carefully around her
She has seen a lot in her sixty-plus years,
But she offers no conversation
Next to her in a crude wooden chair sits her friend
Her hair is black, and her big brown eyes
Are in contrast to Ginger's blue ones
The friend, in a red plaid dress,
Only sometimes repeats a lullaby,
And otherwise speaks not
Friends they have been for many years
Both recently returned from the hospital
Now passing the time side by side
Staring out the window
They would share so many stories
If only they could speak
I wonder what they would tell about me
These two favorite dolls of mine

Sharon Senger
Excelsior Springs, MO

Port Royal

It's so beautiful here
Sitting on the beach
With waves crashing on the shore,
Clear blue skies and hard-packed sand

With the wind whipping through my hair
The salty scent of ocean in my nose
I feel the sea water splash my legs
The gray waves pat my feet

It's as glorious as a shining star here
I never want to leave
The seagulls cawing and pretty shells
Keep me here all day

I walk along the shore to the mound of rocks
Made of granite, sticking out into the water
I climb up to the highest rock
To watch the birds in flight
Fly in crystal skies, not a cloud in sight

I breathe in the warm salty air
Listen to the waves crashing against the rocks
Think of no other thought than where I am now
Port Royal, the place I forever want to stay

Caroline Cole
Buford, GA

Hi, my name is Caroline Cole. I'm from Buford, Georgia, and I love music. My favorite artists are Taylor Swift, One Republic, and Bastille. I also write songs and sing. I got inspiration for this poem from Hilton Head Island, South Carolina. My grandparents own a beach house there in the neighborhood of Port Royal. Since my grandfather has passed on, I decided to honor him by submitting this poem about one of his favorite places on Earth.

Coping

Setting in an ICU waiting room looking at all the faces
A doctor walks in, everyone looks up
Hoping for a good word about a loved one
Impatiently waiting for him to call out a name
It almost seems like a very cruel game
People watching the TV, not really knowing what is on
Suffering and hopefulness to hear, "It's over and they're fine"
You can see the color coming back into their faces
Relief in their eyes, everyone setting there smiles at the person
Hoping to receive those same words, another doctor comes in
Whispered words are exchanged
Tears welling up, running down a face across the room
You know he didn't want to hear those words of gloom
Death is forever, but there is always hope
With all of this you learn to cope

Maggie Flanigan
Sun City Center, FL

I do private duty nursing, so I spend a lot of time in hospitals. That is where my thoughts came from for this poem. I enjoy wood carving so that leaves me time to think of poetry while I'm carving. I enjoy walking and the beach. I really enjoy my job. I love taking care of people, especially seniors. You get so attached to them it is so hard when you lose them. My poetry usually reflects the frame of mind I'm in and writing is a good release for my thoughts.

Clouds

Like the hurricane's blow, I flew home
Over a brown grey miasma, like a dome
Of putrid pollution spreading across the nation
Shore to shore, a harbinger of desolation,
The result of commerce's defecation
On a people helpless in thought.
Through clear separations, white
Thunderheads like cotton balls,
Tombstones for the end of life
In air and water.

Harold Seckinger
Homosassa, FL

I was born on a farm in North Florida in 1926. I'm an architect, musician, writer, painter, sculptor, builder, WWII veteran, and farmer. I'm president of the Citrus Youth Educational Symphonic Orchestra. "The gift of music is the most enriching development of the mind since the beginning of learning." My beginning was the "Depression" and later, memories of war changed that definition. The University of Florida gave me music, a degree in humanities, and a degree in architecture. Eight years of study and work led me to the complexity, people, excitement, art, and beauty in life.

I Will Overcome

The misery of unbelief
can descend to the deepest
labyrinth of the soul
and obscure without any mercy
the longing desires of the innermost.

The misery of unbelief
can transform a sunny sky
into the darkest void
penetrating and succumbing
the fragile and weak mind.

I will rise above the shadows
of misery and unbelief
I will soar like an eagle
to the mountaintop
restore my strength
and pursue the happiness in me.

I will overcome indeed
the misery of unbelief.

A. Grace Maldonado
Port Richey, FL

The Love of My Life

I lost the love of my life,
I lost my beautiful wife.

She was more than just a beautiful girl,
She was my gem, she was my pearl, she was my girl.

We had our disagreements, but they wouldn't linger,
That is because she knew just how to wrap me around her little finger.

She was smart, bright, and witty too,
There wasn't anything, if she tried, that she couldn't do.

I know that time will ease my sorrow,
Maybe next year, maybe tomorrow.

When I think back and wipe away my tears,
I realize we had fifty-five wonderful years.

I know she left this world in God's good grace,
So He will allow her to see His holy and glorious face.

When my life is over and it's time for me to go,
I pray that it's Jesus who comes to take my soul.

I am hoping at the end of life to once again see my lovely wife,
United together in paradise.

Richard Karwoski
St. Louis, MO

Little Baby Ernie

Little baby Ernie,
You were so sweet and so fair
With your mommie's blue eyes,
And your daddy's hair

Such a tiny little mouth
And such a sweet little nose,
Little baby Ernie
You were like a rose

Just a little angel
Sent from Heaven above,
Just a few short days to care for
Just a few short days to love you

Little baby Ernie
With your sweet little smile,
God did not give you to us,
He only lent you for a while

Ollie R. Brunner
Versailles, IN

Forever

Come to one, new memories are made
Leave another, old memories fade away
Return to another, old and new memories are here to stay

Three come together by the sorrowful heart that yearns for joy deeply
A heart is once more pure by togetherness by the solitude heart
Forever love is destiny by the passion of the hopeful heart

Hearts together, stay together by love that is forever
Hearts together, laid to rest together by the light that binds them
Pure light shone and peace is once more by the love that is eternal

Separated once more by war, but wonder to find another and do soon
Together again, fear is replaced with joy
Together again, it ends

Chantell R. Eaton
Interlachen, FL

House Not Home

This house is huge,
double-storied power
meant to look
and feel like money
unnecessary spacious rooms
to feed a god complex
fueled by fear and
overcompensation and
an overwhelming need to feel
accomplished or to just
feel something

Just don't look too close
or you'll begin to see the
fissures separating drywall from
ceiling or baseboard from
wall or feel the chill to
keep the electric bills down
and the bookshelves filled
with posed pictures of
what a family is
meant to look
and feel like before money is
the only end goal

Hannah Bishop
Louisville, KY

Untold

Am I invisible to you
Look at all you put me through
Each night is spent in tears
You only confirm my fears
I put the blade to my skin
The blood drips but through it I grin
The world doesn't know my pain
You do but even you can't keep me sane
I let you into my world—dark and cold
Every secret I had you now behold
Your lies pierce my heart, bleeding red
The tears escape my eyes each night in bed
Silent screams for help unheard
In death I'll fly just like a bird
Do you see me now that I'm gone
My life had ended just as I had drawn
I let the blood ooze from my body at last
The pain ended and my end came so fast
Looking down over you, I can see
You don't shed a single tear for me
The love I gave went unappreciated
Now you live with this secret degraded
I was not the one to kill myself that night
You did when you left after we had that fight
Upon leaving you took my other half
So don't pretend to miss me on your behalf
The world may believe your lies
But I see the truth with my own eyes
Good-bye, my forever

Catera Moody
Cameron, MO

Judge

Question? When you look at me, what do you see?
Do you make your own perception of what you want me to be.
Would you even say I am different because of the way I look or talk,
Maybe my style or even the way I walk.
Could it be where I am from? Or even where I live
Or is it my family? Might be my friends.
If you take a walk in my shoes, or lived one day of my life
Would you still be quick to judge me, or would you think twice?
I have been through heartache and pain, lived through sunshine
and rain.
I have kept my sanity even when I thought I was going insane.
I have been stressed out mentally and physically broken down,
Lost loved ones and close friends every time I turned around.
I thought I was emotionally and intellectually unstable
But I never gave up it was God who kept me able.
So please don't judge me from all the rumors you have heard,
Some of the things that were said was so untrue.
Everyone is different including me from you.
Never judge a book by its cover, at least that's what I thought.
Do not judge me from my appearance try to get to know me
Starting with my heart.

Latrice Randle
Gwynn Oak, MD

Let It Be We

Once it was four,
But there was always we
We once were crossed fingers,
Now look at we
We is no longer a remembrance,
We is so far from recollection,
We is so far it seems impossible
We can still be we if we accept,
We don't need to reason but we need to accept in order to walk
We can't walk down the path if we break arms with wrath
We can't speak if one does not agree to listen,
We can give opinions but one must decide to take it
It can be we again,
This time we make it through without the battle,
This time it can be we if we set aside our disputes,
It can be we if we want it to be
Let be we so we can see,
Let be we so we won't grief
Let it be,
Just let it be

Kayla Alba
Harrison, NY

Words have always been a part of me, even listening to music gives me inspiration. When I focus my mind on a particular matter the ideas just pour through giving me a rush of adrenaline. My father was my inspiration to write this piece. The line "Once it was four, / But there was always we" refers to the four of us in my family, but there was always that closeness between my father and I as we were like "crossed fingers." My father and I have our ups and downs like any other relationship. Some things were difficult to say to my father so I thought what better way to express my point than through a poem.

What

In the end, will we really know
Will it be a friend or foe
Has a life a scheduled end
It's in the book of life, my friend

As one life ends, another will start
To some a burden, others a faulting heart
The November and December of one's life
Problems blossom for a husband and wife

Into the heavens, what a glorious day
Or down to the fire pits, at your dismay
The spirit within you, a golden bell will sound
Believe what you wish, will it be found

Dreaming of stories, that never exist
Memories of events, what an empty list
Forever looking for my place
Searching for acceptance in your face

Facts are known, about our future
Loneliness enters, a needed suture
I'm afraid, you won't be safe, a deeper cut
To protect you I feel has no end, that's what

Gerald Martin Caulfield Jr.
Star Tannery, VA

Death's Accolade:
Testament of a Believing Addict

I die to pain, and die to grief.
I die to shame—hold on belief.
I die to all that offers peace,
And let the lies I told to cease.
So die my-self, and die today.
Give up this fight to hide disgrace.
And in a muffled cry of prayer,
Debate defeat from self-despair.
No longer will I try in vain
To struggle on to win this game.
And as the final flame does dim,
I fall into that silent swim
To give my doubt and fear release,
And give myself—unto Thee.
I count on You to lift me out,
And ask if You could leave the doubt;
The heavy grief with filth and shame,
Replace with hope and life again.
So if to rise up one more morn,
And find that life has still been born;
I'll cry out, and ask to stay
—With You—the battle's end we'll sway.
This verse I cite at day's begin,
And ask that in small ways—we win.
Throughout the day with honest chore,
I'll hope—to live, then pray some more.

Jack Tamplin Jr.
Owenton, KY

Graffiti Youth

They are recluses
Lost to others, but finding themselves
Building their own paths and marching on them
Stomping the grounds of authority
Breaking down all the misery coming their way
They are geniuses
Putting down word after word on the sides of the highway
People scorn, but they continue their ride anyway
They don't care if society doesn't accept them
They think society is a mirage
They've broken through the illusion
Seen the dirt and pain underneath
Turned in their tracks
And learned to live, love, and enjoy
Their time on this wasted Earth

And they watch as society
Comes
crashing
down

Priyanka Ashish Nachane
Livingston, NJ

I have been interested in reading and writing for as long as I can remember. I have always been a different kind of person, who never really fit in with everyone else. "Graffiti Youth" was inspired by my realizing that the teenage mind cannot and should not be constrained as it is in school environments. I am positive that I will never end my love affair with writing. Thank you to those who have supported me and continue to support me along the way. I love you all.

Return to Night

Lying safely here in my bed,
Wrapped in comfort and ease.
Covering all except for my head,
To catch a few more zzz's.

My crocheted blanket is weary and frail,
Generations of love intertwined.
The blocks of colors have now gone pale,
But when daylight starts to shine,

Over my head the blanket goes
To bring back the nighttime sky.
Wrapped in darkness, with pin-prick glows,
Steady, constant, as life spins by.

Constructed with love by angel hands,
With beautiful flaws to be seen.
Unyielding devotion through all my demands,
While here I survive in between.

Krystle Anne McDonald
Topeka, KS

Winter Weather

Winter, winter, snow and white,
hot chocolate a seasonal delight.
Winter, winter, cozy warm clothes,
ice skating, sledding as the wind blows.
Snow balls and children all lined up,
snow men and dogs, hot cider with syrup.
Laughter and singing, church bells ringing,
yesteryear remembered new life springing.
Winter, winter, a special season,
family together for many reasons.
Winter, winter, white as snow,
coming from heaven as you know.
Our hearts cleaned like snow is white,
glowing like Jesus our true light.

David P. King
Falmouth, MA

I was born in California, USA, and moved to Cape Cod, MA, in 2003. I work for the town of Mashpee—DPW—as a custodian. I married my spouse in Vitoria, ES, Brazil. I am an author of many poems waiting for publication opportunities. I'm from an artistic family and married an artist. This poem was inspired by a question given to me online through Publishers Clearing House: "What do you like about winter?" The many activities I experienced over a lifetime of winters were considered in this writing. I hope to become an accomplished writer.

Relief

Do you ever think about just wanting peace?
Turning that stress button off, feeling some relief.

We have to remember that there are people worse off than us.
That's why it's important to take a deep breath.

No more headaches because of bills.
No more feeling your stomach drop because someone just got killed.
No more losing your mind over grief.
So turn that stress button off and feel some relief.

Stella Louise Baldwin
Baltimore, MD

I have been writing since 1979. My poem is about my life and my struggles. Julia and Charles are my parents. Anthony, Allen, Shamika, and Sharea are my children. My love is Rodney. They have all helped to inspire me. I am a person who loves to experience and understand the different cultures of the world. I have traveled to many states and countries. I write because of the gift God gave me and the relief I receive when I put pen to paper. I am hoping my poem will help others and help me achieve my goals.

Red Is Both Good and Bad

Red is the sun
The heat beating down on me
Everyone sips Kool-Aid as they sit by the pool

Red is the color of beauty
Red hair, curly, delicate
Nail polish on my toes still wet

Screaming as blood runs from my cut
The pain is in my eyes
I don't know how anyone can suffer more than this

The words Reed City Coyotes are printed on my paper
Right before the margin line
My pen makes it look stunning

Lava is about to explode from the volcano
People run away so they don't get burned
They yell in rage while their houses are being destroyed

Natalee Morgan Holtz
Reed City, MI

My Headline

I don't watch the news
I find it disturbing
I don't want to know about everything unnerving
I would much rather live in a world of pretend
Where everyone is kind and life has no end
The sadness and mayhem
My heart just can't handle
I prefer to turn it off and light a candle
And pray for the sick and the people in need
Or go out to my garden and plant a little seed
I know life is hard—I am not blind
But I also feel there is so much beauty to find
So for me this is how I choose to live
I want to save my soul so I am able to give
Life is difficult—I know this for sure
But for me I just need to be able to endure
I want to live my life with a light heart
So I am sorry news but I won't let you pierce it like a dart

Noelle Marie White
Arroyo Grande, CA

I am a happily married stay-at-home mom to two daughters. Since becoming a mom, I have become more aware of what is on the news and how my children process it. I wrote this poem to express my disappointment with how the news is presented and my desire to shield my daughters and myself from the negativity.

Stained

Peeking out the door,
seeping through the floor,
the essence of life,
the cause of death.

A heart slowly beating,
a soul softly begging;
the blood has run cold;
a ghost has found its home.

Washed yet remaining, staining,
a story refusing to be ignored.

You close your eyes to unsee the horrors,
but alas! They are screaming your name!

There is no escaping this ghastly haunting:
a story of impulsive desires.

Washed yet remaining, staining:
a story which longs to be told.

Allison E. Schellhorn
Birmingham, AL

Bombs from Hell

Living in a world of joy
Cradling my baby boy
I notice an aching pain in my side
And I must abide.
I hear a joyous sound in the room
And my womb begins to bloom.
And the birth of a new child has taken place.
We celebrate the birth.
But I see what they call an ace.
And every place is in haste
I hear whistling sounds in the sky
And people begin to die.
People say it's because of spies
Or maybe even lies
I hear a cry
And I begin to pry, pry and pry
But I can't get out.
I begin to doubt.
And fingers of fire begin to sprout
Things are burning
People are dying
By now I know
That bombs from hell have commenced
Have taken over.
And the world
Has come to an end.

Jules Faulkner Carr-Chellman
Port Matilda, PA

I dedicate this poem to all the people ever killed in bombings. I also dedicate it to Alison and Davin Carr-Chellman whose fault it was that I have such knowledge. I also dedicate this to Mark Toci who has given me all the common knowledge I need to make it through life. My last dedication is to Colin Chellman who has inspired me to become successful and funny like him. At last, a micro-autobiography: My name is Jules Carr-Chellman. I live in State College, PA. I am a Boy Scout in Troop 375. I love the internet, video games, people, food, and social events.

The Reasons

A letter, a word, a sentence
I read.
There's something specific you imply that
I need.

The voices, the music, the humming
You hear.
A time zone, a preference, a necessity
You fear.

Our life lines, our stories, our hearts
We share.
Our wishes, our dreams, our hopes
We care.

A feeling, a look, a sound
They know.
A smile, a laugh, a cry
They show.

The lightness, the darkness, the blurry grey
We see.
The reason we live, we spend our days here:
To be.

Gina Munro
Denver, CO

Please, Go Gently

When I think of the frigid wind
that will one day carry my soul
over hills blanketed in green
and through valleys donning gowns of flowers
I think of you as well;
you are the only one
whose essence I wish the wind to embrace with warmth
and I hope that perhaps it decides
for you both to linger over the rolling landscape
that embodies pure serenity
so as to grant you one last glance
at the beautiful earth you only recently graced
with the last heave of your tired lungs.
I do wish your soul to refrain from deserting your body
for as long as humanely possible;
though when the algid lips of death
graze your ghostly cheek
and the breath of the trees
and the grass
and the flowers takes you
I pray it be gentle while caressing all that you once were.

Emily Cortese
Lake Hopatcong, NJ

Frigid

Winter engulfs
An increasingly weakening being.
As the grass transforms into pallid stalks
So doth this soul metamorphose:
  On its skin
  Blooms a toxic frost.

As the snow bruises
Defeated blades of green,
So fades this consciousness
  To malignant indigo
  Suffocated by a sky
  Poised for retribution.

What creature is this,
This vengeful sky?

It is I, and I
Am that
Persecuted earth
Wounded by the wind and
Mangled by mankind.

Marjorie Beryl Wisler
Sturgis, MI

This is the story of one human who has abandoned the idea of warmth, a human, wounded by this world, who shattered into an apathetic heap, only to be dealt one final, lethal, icy blow to the soul. This is the story of one human whose own villain is herself: she is infatuated with the seasons, though for her, they only ever breathe bitter animosity.

The Element of Love

For your eyes are as bright as shining metal,
But your eyes have a softer touch than that.
For gorgeous metal is put on a mantle,
Or tracked in to be wiped off on a mat.
But your eyes symbolize our love—pure.
My love is more pure than titanium,
For all despair has but one true cure.
My heart exploded my uranium,
But none of the elements can kill love.
For our love is as bright as a fire,
And our love was brought by a pure white dove.
Cupid aimed at us and pulled the wire,
The arrows that he fired we both caught.
All our friends thought no—that is but a thought.

Collin Patrick Romero
Albuquerque, NM

Love Everlasting

He is not coming.
As much as I beg and I plead, I scream to the heavens.
I imagine the moment my eyes meet his.
He lifts me from the ground into his arms, yet speaks not a word.
He has come for me!
But he is *not* coming, and the dream is dead. Part of me is dead.
Part of me is beaten up. Part of me is split wide open.
Naked to the air, yet unable to catch my breath.
But only for a moment. Then, I find *it,* deep down inside of me.
I rejoice. I twirl around within his arms, yet he's not here.
In the memories, he is, and he forever will be. For he is my love.
He is me. I am him. That love is alive.
Permanently living inside me. No one, not even he, can take it away.
He doesn't have to be here with me, and I feel it.
I am it, the love is inside me. It takes no form.
It is not him... not his physical body pressed against mine.
Not his pounding heart to my ear, as we embrace.
Not the words of, I love you.
It is the energy that exists from our souls' connection,
And it is still so alive. It never dies, because it is love.
That love will guide me forever. I will revel in it.
I will cherish and protect it, for all my days.
It is a fire inside of me, that keeps me warm and safe. It is real.
With no idea how it got there, or why it should be there.
It *fills* me.
Finding myself in the true presence of love, it has *become* me.
Yet denied me...
He is not coming.

Trisha M. Endaz
Shrewsbury, MA

Guardian

She took a heart made out of cold
She took the heart and made it gold
She took some caution, when leaving love
Yet one day had been really tough
She tried to warm a frozen heart
He stole her love, broke her apart
She couldn't love… she couldn't think
This type of healing no one can bring
She fell away into a hole
And then became extremely cold...
And so they say many hearts she froze
When she became the one they loathe
They hated her guts, they hated her skin
They would not stop hating, through thick and thin
And so she fell into a spiral...
Until she was saved by one admirer
It was the cold-hearted beast that once had been hated
They shared bad times, but then they dated
He loved her so much and followed her ways
Of warming a heart it took many days
But one day she awoke, she laughed and smiled
She screamed to the world, "I am alive!"
The two went on to fight for lives
To help one another through very tough times
And though it was hard the love prolonged
If you love someone, please stay strong!

Elizabeth Michelle Lirner
Brooklyn, NY

Euthanasia

One day I will grow old
I will have physical challenges
day to day
I will struggle
but I don't want euthanasia
yes, I'm dying softly
aren't we all?
euthanasia is not for me
you see no matter how many challenges I face
I will shine like a blossoming flower in spring
I want you to listen to me
euthanasia will not kill me
I will conquer this
I would rather suffer than be free
from my pain if it means I can't see your face again
I would cause you so much pain
I see those tears in your eyes
please wipe them away
euthanasia is not for me
I will always love you darling baby
always
God is the author and finisher of my faith
so no man can bother me
therefore euthanasia get away from me

Angelika Maria Lowder
Tallahassee, FL

I Will Still Love You

I will still love you,
Even when the hidden is sought by name,
For my hands are clean and new.

Cast to drift in an ocean of blue,
The result of misfortunate aim
But, I will still love you.

Skipping with angels of few,
The white surface became consumed by red flames,
For my hands are clean and new.

Stooped in front of the pew
Your emotions became hard to tame.
I will still love you.

The angels pointed to,
Yet you lay there lame,
For my hands are clean and new.

A frosted carnation silently flew
While your eyes focused on the fame.
I will still love you,
For my hands are clean and new.

Kristen Birstok
Pembroke Pines, FL

Home

In the end when the hope is gone
and life's too hard to continue on,
when eyes are dead and souls are weak,
bodies hurt, spirits meek,
when in our hearts we're all alone,
how do we find our way back home?

Kimberly Ann Copper
North Platte, NE

Lori's Garden: A Touch of Heaven

As a dazzling diamond
tiara captivates all who
see it,
So the technicolor parade
of beauties in Lori's garden
Hypnotizes the lucky eyes
that happen by.
They see a floral rainbow
That freely gives the gifts
of beauty, color, serenity,
and awe....

Gwendolyn Wade
St. Louis, MO

Helium

99 red balloons
Or so that's what he will sing
High pitched kisses
Sucked and sipped through licorice lips

He will say commitment scares him
Like the echo from metal barrels
Like growing orchids from dewy marrow

He will say commitment scares him
But his arm is sleeved with sharp charcoal ink
Of three-leaf clovers and Darwin-noted birds

And I will try to drown my butterflies in vodka
So their wings stop fluttering
Inside bone cages

Marinated by the high
Burning in liquid transparency
This was comatose
From empathy

Good night like yesterday

Garrett Young
Alameda, CA

Born and raised in the Bay Area, I came into writing at a later age, after my passion for art. I attend San Francisco State University as a creative writing major, hoping to make my pieces memorable to my readers. My main goal is to evoke empathy between the speaker and reader. I hope for the ability to touch someone with my craft and to move the individual through an internal journey. Enjoy helium, breathe it in, and watch it fade out like the relationship of the poem.

Let's Be Stars

Let's brag about our future
How we're going to save the world
How we're going to fly high and smile
At the others below

Let's make a living in the skies as we glow
Because indeed our location will be dark,
But we'll make our own lights
Oh, we'll be spectacular,
They'll think of us when they see great lights
Illuminating great mics like the sun

And the kids will unleash a burst of energy as they run
And scream out, "Look up there Mommy!"
Oh, we'll be great
They won't be able to catch us
For we'll be faster than the wilds of the forest

We don't need to rest
We'll never know what movie they put us in
Or what music we're forced to play in so he can win the girl's heart
Nor the melody that made kids realize what we are

But it don't matter because we're stars
Don't you see we're already too high to be pulled towards the low?
I promise you, it won't be fun
It will burn to even live because this will put you to the test
But we'll make the best of what we have like the reckless in a car
We're blue giants living fast and dying young.

Charles Joseph Augustin
Brooklyn, NY

Clear Being

And in my life of black and white
Your heart was beating red
And in my sea of misery
I remembered what you said

Your eyes had been empty
And mine had been blind
But our vision is clear now
And so is my mind

Averie Grace Severs
Barrie, ON

Averie Severs is the author of the poem "Clear Being." She is an amateur writer who enjoys writing contemporary pieces. "Clear Being" is about the little things that help pull you out of your darkness. It may be someone's love or maybe the words of wisdom they have shared with you. They help you clear your vision and your mind, and with those two aspects you can become further aware of your self purpose.

The Lord Started Speaking

Find yourself my child I say
I have a plan for you everyday
You are great no matter what people say
Listen to me, I'll lead the way
I'll order your steps day by day
Don't look to the left or to the right
Remember faith is not by sight
Lean not to your own understanding
Life can be very demanding
Ask me things that you know not
I will give you prophetic insight
I have gifts prepared for you
Spiritual and natural too
Search for me and you will find
I've been there the whole time

Regina Hughes Bruce
Northport, AL

Asleep I Thought

this morning I woke up with a cut on my finger and thought
how did I get this little cut on my finger I thought
I must have been on such an adventure asleep I thought
last night tucked under six or seven comforters (because I get cold

at night) and I thought where and what had I been
under those comforters last night to earn me such a mark I thought
that little cut now turned a hazy pink under healing flesh so
it must've been a long long time ago I thought for such an adventure
so I must have fallen into a nest of a vulture or tumbled

aimlessly into a serpent's lair with glimmering carapace or awoken
a dragon and drew my sword and in a mutually terrified excitement
we slew our differences and split a pipe of rich red wine and
frolicked together to the sound of a single white drum until the wine
spilled all over my
six or seven comforters I thought and now

looking at this little cut on my finger I'm desperately wishing
that I was more interesting

Amanda Friedlander
Bozeman, MT

I'm just an average college student who still sleeps with a teddy bear and eats stale ramen noodles with sriracha for two out of three meals per day. This is for my parents, Gary and Wendy Friedlander, who taught me to "rise above" and to keep writing, keep dreaming and keep fighting until there's nothing left but words on paper. This is for my love, Max, who looks at my crazy, jumbled mess of a mind and kisses it until everything makes sense again. Thank you all for never giving up on me.

Dropped Camera Playback

Sidewalk, sideways,
paved ground right, morning sky left,
left behind—recording in progress.

Stiletto (first-day professional),
skinny straps, clack slap,
concrete crack eats heel, stumble off to work.
Brick edges crumble red,
stretch to sky; terra-cotta, cracked side, green rot,
no plants, rainbow of chewed gum
floating in old rain.

Sun peaks in the sky—
orthopedic sneakers (white),
dress shoes (polished),
bruised flip flops,
combat boots (laced halfway),
worn-down soles, lonely.

Streetlights switch, whine,
flicker while sun still lingers.
Broken high heels return,
stiletto clack slap (avoid the crack),
pink blisters, raw,
in motion, then gone.

Laura Elizabeth Renshaw
Chapel Hill, NC

The Man in the Mirror

I wake up this morning and who do I see,
But a man in the mirror, staring at me.
Who is this man that stares back at me,
Is it a reflection, what do I see?
He says that he knows me from long time ago,
He does look familiar, the more that I know.
I'm afraid to look in, afraid what I'll find,
He says with a smile, know me it's time.
The reflection is clear, the more that I see,
The reflection of God staring at me.
He says with a smile, it's been quite some time,
Welcome back, I miss you my child.
My eyes swell with tears, for I'm happy to see,
The God that's within smiling at me.
The reflection is gone, the man now I see,
Is someone I know, a man who's at peace.
It's easy to change the person within,
Just look in the mirror and accept with a grin.
The reflections the same for woman or man,
The reflection of God, the reflection of man.

George Charles Velasco
Miami, FL

Vases

It's crystal like vases
Running in worries of different cases.
Dry cold turns to cold,
And yet no warmer of a day to settle in
  Upturned—
It's not the urn but instead a welling up of
Springs wishing to make the trees dance again if only
In a hush till the laces call the wintry spiders home.

Erika Lynne Sten
Averill Park, NY

Broken

My chamber is an empty cell cold and miserable,
the sounds of sorrow steady lingers on the walls.
A foundation unstable with cracks and erosion
a faint beat can barely be heard.
Where did all the laughter go what happened to the light
what crumbled those impenetrable walls
what dismantled that foundation that was stronger than life.
Was it the wind was it the rain
was it the earth or a scorching flame
or was it the thing that created it that brought it to its knees.
(Love)

Robert Murphy
Columbus, OH

Lesson to the Learned

They carve a place for you
in the echoes of dead men's books.
Listening with a tasteful ear,
you filter truths
as Whitman said to do
and make your place among the frequencies.
'Tis not enough,
in this pulse of flesh, to make truth,
for without happiness,
We slowly starve.

He forgot in his leaves to say
his secret to harvesting your own happiness,
to originally shine, reflection-less.

        Just do.
Beat on;
run sparkling into the heart of the world,
wild.

Gina Ferrantelli
Highland Mills, NY

To Wonder in Love

In the sea holds the land
on that land holds my heart
within my heart is my hand
and in my hand is yours.

In your eyes I see me
and me and you were meant to be
like the sea to the land
like a hand for a hand
and like my heart for yours.

Lisa Marie Roth
Petersburg, WV

Thoughts

No matter how far you are, you are always
in my thoughts. I wish to be your good
night, as you my good morning. Let the
stars shine bright upon you, as I wish you
to fall into the sweetest of dreams. Anxiously
waiting for the sunrise to pierce through
the cracks of your window, giving
you a heavenly awakening and a
smile for the rest of your day.

Adrian Acosta
Hialeah, FL

Last Word

Her ghost permeates it all.
She was the first.
Cancer called her home a
decade passed.
Her vision of Christ coming to her
famously told over and over.
Her last words: "He is alive to me."

Her children and you grew.
My new groom, history untold,
called her name in the night.
Fifteen years: they moved on.

Your last words, "You are dead to me."

In the dark woods,
strangers intend no contact.
Eyes averted,
my path crosses no one.
My ghost permeates it all
the past echoing my name.

My last words…

Karen Ann Hookway
Buffalo, NY

Beginning

So quickly, from the start that we now barely do recall,
Our long ascent to the peak seems so clear to all
Though blinded at times by the rugged roads taken,
Lest forgetting the struggles and urges to be forsaken

Time for a break and long glance below,
Such warmth and pride though their pace seems so slow
Trying so hard to guide and tell of the way,
Now hidden from our eyes, their path to us seems to stray

Returning to the task and unknowns still ahead,
We march up through storms with nothing to dread
What lies over that crest is a mystery yet to reveal,
However, the trek is once again the great appeal

Oh so near, do we follow the trail so straight,
Or veer our way before it may be too late
Now out of breath from the choice we make,
To our amazement the summit is only a rest to take

The distant view ahead selects our way,
As we again step just like that first day
Oft reminding each as we need to hear,
The pleasure is the journey and the beginning is so near!

Thomas Lopez
Germantown, TN

Crystal, My Favorite Nurse

When the day comes,
And your job is done,
I'll miss you,
That's for sure,
But friends we'll be,
I knew you see,
The first day you walked through our door.
You're very special,
And you have a gift.
Awesome care is what I got,
You're kind, caring and so much more.
I'm very blessed,
To have met a wonderful person like you.
You were sent by God,
That's for sure,
Because taking care of me,
I know was a chore.

Debbie Cherene Wagner
Muncy, PA

This is dedicated to an amazing lady: Crystal Lichty. In November of 2014, I had my second major surgery. God sent an angel to care for me; her name is Crystal, and she has a special gift. Crystal not only tends to your physical needs, she also knows just what to do to help you deal with the emotional turmoil that goes along with recovery, and she always keeps your spirits up! I thank God for sending this wonderful lady to care for me. If only all nurses had Crystal's qualities. Crystal is very special, every day she makes a difference!

Ronnie

A smile, crinkles by his eyes
Chasing two little girls around a backyard
A ladybug lands and he tells them how special it is

From then on the girls always treasured the sight
Never once taking for granted the words he told them
They were much younger then, but now they understood
This was to be theirs to treasure not for just now but forever

A man, popping his hip out, talking in a high pitched voice
The sound coming from the kitchen, the girls would pop their
heads in
He'd joke about acting out the role of his female counterpart

Back then they would look at one another and be confused
But once they were a bit older they learned he just was having fun
They started to realize that he was fitting in with the girls
Always one to act a fool, but would call himself out before you could

A man, touching the hearts of those close to him
He was a father, a brother, an uncle
Yet more importantly a husband

The two girls always saw and understood the love he had for his wife
The woman who he'd chosen to spend the rest of his life with
He loved her truly and it touched their hearts when he left
But he loved her even past his last breath

Jordan Lyn Perry
Medford, MA

My Dream Girl

My dream girl is perfection,
But she had flaws that I could adore.
My dream girl is challenging,
But she made me want to be more.
My dream girl is caring,
But she made me smile every day.
My dream girl is funny,
But she was obscene in every way.

My dream girl is ambitious,
But she could not make simple decisions.
My dream girl is honest,
But she was careful of having collisions.
My dream girl is respectful,
But she was not best friends with my mother.
My dream girl is sexual,
But she could perform like no other.

My dream girl is generous,
But gifts were not all she gives to me.
My dream girl is gorgeous,
But that's not why we are meant to be.
My dream girl is in my future,
But not just the house on the beach,
Kids too.
My dream girl is…
My dream girl was you.

Mathew Gullotta
Sydney, NSW

Smoke Clouds

when the smoke clears
people don't forget
the blood doesn't stop flowing
the pain doesn't stop
the dead are still dead
mothers have lost sons
sons have lost fathers—sisters their brothers
war… it breaks families destroys lives
and little boys become men who run to war
and we clap… but not the little girl
not the little girl who lost
her father and her brother
not the woman who loses
her son and husband
it's all over the news
we won! we won!
yeah we won
but we lost… we lost people
how… how will she tell them
tell them their father is gone
that their father is dead
so clap
clap because we won
but remember the little boys and girls
because when the smoke clears
people don't forget

Jourdan J. Collins
Plano, TX

Thoughts for My Sleeping Wife

I find you in your new skirt. Sleep
has usurped your best intentions.
Nemesis. Nymph. Friend.
Faint breeze in curtains wheels
the afternoon in spangles
across bed and wall—game figures
wandered to cheeks and lashes, earthy fingers
curled in the act of clasping or release.

I wonder if you would know me here.
Accidental brush of hair or lips
could start you from miles of rippled grass,
stiff sailed clouds, palominos nuzzling
strands, forehead laid in drowsy clover.
That meadow I once burned, or tried to, you said.
I can't return. Or don't know how.

You stir and the breeze falls back again.
Still small fires return in their cycle
passing like stars across your eyes.
I recognize you now, would know you if
you woke imperfect and inculpable
ready to speak the few good words,
hoping you're still mine.

David W. Parsley
Azusa, CA

Concrete Love

love is fleeting
and she found that she was not wrong in the way she loved
with all her heart
but wrong in loving people
who bear both the capability and the tendency to leave
she learned it was better to love the things that were concrete
so she loved the mountains in the distance
and the books on her bookshelf
she loved the moon and its neighboring stars
and the sea and its crashing waves
the fault lied not in the method but in the object
so she loved those lasting things with all her heart
and she shut the rest of the world away,
when she was ready to try love again
she found that fear had left a lock on the door she had shut
but she loved what she could with all that she had left to give

Hannah Elizabeth Barrett
Celina, TX

Eternal Student

hungry for knowledge
learning from pain
never-ending chapters
I am the eternal student

Lacy M. Eckhardt
Phoenix, AZ

America

America is blessed by God and His
holiness people praise Him day and
night 'cause we love Him and He listens
to our prayers and we are thankful for Him
He praises family and friends then
we are fast asleep and He praises Him

Anaiya Meikle
Cutler Bay, FL

My name is Anaiya Meikle Jurine. I live with my mom, dad and brother. I am from Jamaica. I go to Whigam Elementary School. I am a model, dancer and a writer. This is a big opportunity for me. I am from Jamaica, but live in Miami. My aunt and mom inspired me to write this wonderful poem because every once in a lifetime there is this big opportunity that you feel will change your life forever.

Fall

Fall is where the leaves turn gold and brown
All the leaves fall to the ground
Love is still in the air from summer flings
Love is nipping at your nose with the frost

Kenneth Edward Leyhe
Pasadena, MD

Over the Hill

I get almost to the top but still can't see
What is there over the hill for me.
In the distance I see a dark stormy sky,
Will it mean troubles and make me cry?
There are also patches of lovely blue I see,
Does that mean pleasures and happiness for me?
The sun peaks out with a golden glow
And high above floats a glorious rainbow.
What a variety of sights are in my view,
The beauty, the glory and darkness too.
I guess that I'm just not meant to see
What waits there, over the hill for me.

Betty Gallimore
Phoenix, AZ

Notion of Home

Home is not a place or gilded space
or a vainglorious effusion constructed upon a lake
Neither is it a cardboard shelter built within the park
poor decimated souls surviving the translucent dark
Home is the solid foundation that lies deep within
it encourages us to grow, it compels us to win
Home is not the stuff of misplaced dreams
nor a heavenly venue where golden angels sing
Home is the steady hand that calms the night
its brilliance so illuminating, it turns darkness to light
Home is the rare inclination, we seldom ever find
an outmoded misconception, a false promise eludes the mind
Home is the one you love, protected within your arms
cherish the love that radiates, beneath your open palms
Some say it's a mythical notion, assuredly they are wrong
maybe home is just a quiet place, a place where you belong
To design this concept of home, just a reminder where to start
a home is not a home, until it's built inside your heart

Donnell Perryman
Reno, NV

They Say That Time

They say that time,
you blink,
it's gone.
And I'd suppose
that's right,
for those,
who rush and
run and
wish away.
But time, you see,
this passing time,
will wait.
Here,
on the edge of the
wooded planks.
Where,
time is kept by
changing tides.
Where,
sun meets sea in
vital bursts.
As salted waves
caress the hours,
until time,
time is but a notion for
some other day.

Jillian Catherine Manning
Andover, MA

Racism

Dehumanizing, demoralizing, filled with hate
and dirty little lies,

I cry for the life that has passed me by, being penalized
and held back simply because, I am black and proud.

Visualizing my forefathers and the vicious attacks,
snatched my history from me, hard to get it back.

Left many strange fruit hanging from the tree in the
process, like the evil that Cain possessed.

You left many Indians slain as well with the force
of your brutality.

Why can't you just let me be, set me free from your
cruel delusions of what my life, should be;

a tear shed, mourning my dead, yet you still fail to
see what your irrational behavior does to me,

instead my pain incites you to take pride and feel
justified in your evil deeds.

Can you verbalize why that is?

Connie Jordan
Sacramento, CA

Connie Jordan, troubled by the things seen in the world, with no true platform, turned to poetry as a means of expression with her first book release, The World Through a Poet's Eyes, *in 2015. This poem was created based on her witnessed and experienced racism in America—simply because of the skin color being black. A hard journey, but she survived because of the strength she found inside, the love she received from God and the peace she found in Jesus. Peace be with you on your journey.*

Freedom Of

It's such a relief to know
I can say exactly
What I want to say
To you.

I need not wrap my words like packages,
Fussing over ribbons and bows.
My thoughts aren't delicate.
I can throw them against the wall
Or drop them down the stairwell
And they'll reach your ears just the same.

I can sob or scream or
Whisper
And you'll know what I mean.

In the moments I am with you, my soul can breathe.
You free me so that I can be precisely who I want
And need
To be.

Rachel Griebel
Hoagland, IN

For My Family

I don't live in a mansion
Have no diamond wedding band
Not even one crumpled dollar
To crinkle in my hand

First it was five children
They were really cute
Sometimes us Maiers added
Water to our soup

Our kids grew and time flew
Now we have nine grandkids too
They went to school, finished college
Enjoyed life with their new knowledge

Time kept marching on
Happiness every way
Now we have six great-grandkids today

Grandma sits in her rocking chair
Many memories and gray hair
Put up the wreaths—decorate the tree
How much happier can this life be

Thank you children in all you do
You make all my dreams come true

Rose Maier
Massillon, OH

"For My Family" was inspired by my own family. My deceased husband, Johnnie, and I had five children, nine grandchildren and eight great-grandchildren. I am eighty-three years old and have also written a "Maier Family History" book. Every Christmas, holiday, birthday or special occasion, I enjoy writing poems and stories to honor them.

I Fell

I fell down and scraped my knee
But that's okay
I had a hand stretched to me

I fell off my bike and began to cry
But that's okay
I heard my name and no good-bye

I fell so far I couldn't see
But that's okay
I found a light inside of me

I fell off my swing and onto the ground
But that's okay
I felt strong arms wrap me around

I fell down and bonked my head
But that's okay
I know a man who took stripes of red

I fell on the stairs because I couldn't catch the rails
But that's okay
I have a friend who took three nails

Robert Gordon
Boise, ID

One in the Same Revisited

Imagine as I stand before you, no flesh upon you or me,
How exactly would you feel, what exactly would you see?
The undercoat of innocence we will share upon that day.
As once before, the flesh no more our soul is into play.
And would you be a human of habit and bring your life to shame.
And not want to be a part of me, for our soul is not the same.
The point that I'm trying to make and sadly still rings true,
The difference that you see my brother—is the difference within you.
I wrote these words years ago, for my grandchildren, soon to be.
For I had heard a man in '63—speak of life and equality.
The words that he spoke were strong and steady
And received by those with might.
But still what lingered in the past "not without a fight"
You could hear the silent echo "what exactly do you mean"
The strength in word from a man not heard because he has a dream?
My prayer is still the same my friends
Our conflict we must tame.
For you and me will always be, truly, one in the same.
I'm your brother, your sister a child of God and we are one in
the same.

Lorie Brennan
Jacksonville, AR

Perhaps in Her Dreams She Does Remember

Last week they came in droves: children, grandchildren and great-grandchildren. How thrilled she was that whole day!
But…
Mama doesn't remember.

Next morning came a surprise visitor, Melinda. "I'm here for breakfast, Nana." That same afternoon, Allison called. "I am nearby. Thought you'd like some company. I brought the wool you were looking for."
But…
Mama doesn't remember.

Next day, lunch with her daughter Phoebe, Betty, her cousin, and her brother, whom she adores, with Sonia, our cousin. Dinner, the same day: Barby and Matty bring food. Mama says, "You're the best son-in-law, also a good cook."
But…
Mama doesn't remember.

Two days later, Jon and Jamie arrive with a package in hand. "It's a telephone, Nana. You'll get used to the buttons. Rotary is so old-fashioned. I'll install it for you."
But…
Mama doesn't remember.

It's my day for visiting, trying to get Mama to leave her house and go shopping. She's getting smaller, frailer, more stubborn. Yet, she's always happy to see me. I say, "You had a busy week. The whole family visited. Wasn't it wonderful?" She says, "I had company? Tell me. Tell me. Who was here?"
But
Mama doesn't remember.

Gloria Sussman
Boynton Beach, FL

A Better Me

Here I sit in a chair
of wooden sand.
And so I ponder my
future.
Wondering where do I go
from here?
I am but a drop of rain
in a cloud of storms.
Don't let me dry up before
my cloud of storms
passes.
I am not the clumsy
child you painted me.
I am complex deep dark
and insightful.
I am made of many colors.
Let my rainbow shine,
As I begin my new journey.
It's yet a new endeavor.
All I want to do is help
people, take care of them.
Will you let me do that?

Annie Devore
Seminole, FL

Circles

There is a circus in me
And in this circus
I am a tiger
I am a tiger who knows
How to escape
The confines of her cage
But I never stray far
For some odd reason
And I find myself caught
Clawing for a while
Until I realize
That I am clawing
At my own stripes
The same stripes I curse
And admire the lion's mane
Though I am freer than her
I suppose we all suffer this pain
There is a circus in me
And in this circus
I am a tiger
Dancing through circles of fire
Desiring greater purpose
Could I be the courage
I require to desert this?
Granting myself worth is
Dancing into freedom

Candace Sheppherd
Los Angeles, CA

The Monster under My Bed

For as long as I can remember I have been terrified at night.
Nightmares have always consumed me and I couldn't wait 'til the morning light.
Even when I was three years old I dreamt of that ugly face.
He told me he would kill me if I failed to win the race.
Every night I tried and tried to beat him to the door
And every night I was too slow just like all the nights before.
Each time I turned the knob I saw his evil grin…
He would yell, "I've got you," and it would start all over again.
I didn't stand a chance because I was not allowed to run…
He made me crawl upon my knees… he laughed and had his fun.
Most children think there are monsters underneath their bed
And their parents assure them that it's all in their head.
But the monster in my room, he wasn't just a dream
And no matter how hard I tried I never could break free.
The monster that came into my room was evil, sick, and bad.
And the worst part is (I'm ashamed to say) the monster's name was Dad.
His job was to protect me from the evil in this world.
He should have never done the things he did to his little girl.
It's a secret I've kept hidden way down deep inside
It will affect every relationship I have until the day I die.
So if your little one is afraid of the dark, understand the way they feel.
Because sometimes the monsters under their bed are real…

Melissa A. Manning
Chickasha, OK

Resilience

I woke up today to see
a quite whole different me,

a girl that is making better choices
someone that is living free

in a world with no more pain
workin' like I've got something to gain.

Today, I'm feeling just a little bit lucky,
family and friends no longer trying to "duck me."

I want to do right,
each new day and every night

I'm waking up early
and I'm seeing the light

the past is the past
and I gave up the fight.

I'm going to walk down my street
and greet each person I meet

with my chin in the air
no looking down… nothin' to see there.

I've picked myself up before
and I'll do it again

'cause my life—once a struggle
I thought I'd never win.

So, now it's time to define
the whole "new" me

—priorities re-arranged
to show the world how great I can be.

Angela Fulk
Howell, MI

O' Love O' Love

how could you leave me now,
your slave your fool your
minion, to be mocked
shunned and ridiculed by those
with wasted opinions, perhaps
they know not of you their lives
you haven't touched, then
search must they if they're to
know this feel this thrill this
heaven's touch, I remember when
you came to me in a park
beneath trees so shady, so
many years have past since then
o' I must have counted eighty,
don't leave me now I beg of thee
don't let my heart turn cold,
o' love o' love don't leave me now
not now that I am old

Raymond Washington
East Orange, NJ

Suede the Dog

I love my dog Suede, he is towards the end.
I will miss him again and again.
He is my favorite dog, he is such a good friend.
I will miss him again and again.
He has big brown eyes, just like me,
and we both like lunch meat; our favorite is bologna.
He loves his bed that I did buy,
I will miss him when he dies.
He just turned 13, in human life.
I'll be 10 on Christmas night.
I hope he makes it till that time,
because he's such a good friend of mine.
I'm really going to miss him, until time ends.
I'm going to miss him over and over again and again.

Emyah Green
Mt. Morris, NY

Kisses in the Sky

Did not know I would feel this bad
Did not know I could feel this sad
Since that day we said good-bye
I have sent you a million kisses in the sky

You were the best part of every day
I do not know why they took you away
Maybe someday I'll know the reason why
But until then my loves, I'll send kisses in the sky

My heart aches for you each and every day
My mind drifts with thoughts of you far away
Thinking you'll forget me makes me cry
Knowing that all I can do is send kisses in the sky

I hope they realize soon that we should be together
For me that's the only thing that will make my life better
So until this sad time passes by
Please catch Grandma's kisses in the sky

Marianne DiFiore
Staten Island, NY

Dearest Shamrock Taylor Swift

Dearest shamrock Taylor Swift,
You're like a four-leaf clover on St. Patrick's day.
Remember our secret passage in Paradise Cove years ago in the country of
Canada where we first kissed at Dunkirk Lighthouse at Veterans Museum at
69 Point Gratiot in New York state NY?
It's where we got married remember then? Dearest shamrock Taylor Swift in 2015.

Stephen J. McCarthy
Fairborn, OH

Fairy Tales

The other night I had a dream about Cinderella, Snow White, and all of those Walt Disney movies.
I was the heroine and you were my prince in white shining armor.
You rode up on your silvertip horse, and with your razor sharp sword, stabbed me fatally in my romantic heart.
I repeated the phrases about submissive surrender… the ones that the man in the black frock pronounced so clearly.
I became your slave, your bedmate, a happy ending… until a nightmare disturbed my sleep, and you rode off with Goldilocks.

Linda Fry
Lexington Park, MD

When Death Comes for Me

When Death comes for me, it will be a relief.
No more lonely days, or nights filled with grief.
My children don't come see me or call to chat,
Most of the time, it's just me and my cat.
I'll see them at Christmas or birthdays,
But other than duty visits that is that.
I only go out to see doctors and such,
My quality of life really isn't much.
I have a husband I love who also loves me,
But most days, he spends watching TV.
I read, or I write, sometimes I sew,
But do I get to travel, the answer is no.
I'd like to go out to dinner and a dance.
I'm told I'm not able so there is no chance.
My home is paid for free and clear,
So is my car, and I have food and clothes.
But I'd like to join a gym to exercise and swim.
I'm told I wouldn't go, so that isn't in.
Why get my hair done when it doesn't last a day,
As for a manicure or pedicure, there's no way.
Maybe I'll start back going to the Catholic Daughters,
But the meetings are at night and getting rides is a bother.
I'm laying here now, unable to sleep.
It's 3 AM, what hours I keep.

Joyce Taylor-Smith
Spring, TX

Now at Age 82

Now at age 82:
Oh! How those years flew.
One by one I saw them shine,
All those dreams that were all mine.
I know my dreams are not complete,
But oh! the challenges I did meet.

My working days now in the past,
I am retired at last!
I'm in my third trimester, I've been told;
In other words I'm really old.

But, one big thing I still can do is get up at dawn to meet with friends,
'Cause I have some ears to bend
A visit with people who have touched my heart;
Then wait for bingo to start.
We'll share a smile, coffee, maybe a snack,
We wait for the caller to get back.

Then the caller's voice rings out:
"Good morning all, is this your first bout?
Bingo is starting, let us pray;
This might be your lucky day!"
My one big question on my mind:
Is there a bingo god to find?
And if there is, why does he hide?
I really need him by my side.

Phyllis Bishop Montero
Manteca, CA

Mirror

I look at her.
I stare at her blonde, wavy hair and her shallow, upside-down smile. I stare deep down into her lonely, grey eyes.
I barely recognize her.
I see her every day, but I don't know who she is. I never really cared who she is.
She means nothing to me, but yet somehow, she means so much.

Some days she's beautiful: skin radiating, eyes back to blue, so happy and peaceful.
But most days she's ugly; her reflection is her worst enemy.
I look at her with great interest: studying her, observing her every move. The way she slouches when she walks. The way she looks at the ground when she talks.
I wonder if others see her the way I do.

What is beautiful?
The love between a mother and her daughter? A newborn baby?
The perfect melody? What about Earth itself?
I don't know. Does anyone?
I judge her when I see her: every morning and every night when I look in the mirror.
Each day is different, but in reality, I never change.

Briauna Zimmer
Kalamazoo, MI

Therapy

I had finally agreed to do what I knew I had to do
to help myself,
but didn't feel any better for it.
In fact I felt much worse
as the reality weighed down heavily upon my shoulders
and what heart I had left
sunk down to my toes
seeping slowly into the floor and away.
Now what remains?
A hollow, desolate creature
with a past as turbulent as the raging sea,
but no future.
The only thing ahead of me is this cage—
golden and good,
one I cannot escape
like the room I'm in now
which seems to be closing in around me
the door out getting farther and farther away
until I'm left wondering
if I can ever reach it.
And still the voice drones on,
unwilling to let me go.

Miriam L. King
Prescott, WI

This poem emerged when the hero in a novel I was writing at the time must attend psychological therapy and I realized the thought-provoking prose could be put to verse. My former poetry has been featured in a local coordinated art-and-literary exhibit. I have been the winner of a national short fiction award and was also selected to write a play that was performed by a distinguished theater company. From a young age, I loved creating stories and my greatest aspiration has been to share those stories with others. My hope is to be a published novelist.

Scars

Can't erase the lines
Caged animal crying out
Scars exhibition

Jennifer Lynn Wall
Severn, MD

Heavy Hearts

There they stand with heavy hearts,
Knowing they will be far apart.
He is leaving to fight a war,
Won't be back 'til their son turns four.
He can't help but hold her close,
For she is the one he loves the most.
There is nothing else to say,
She will miss him every day.
This is no time to be shy,
This could be their last good-byes.
He tells her, "I love you!"
She replies, "I do too!"

See Her-Coogan
Eau Claire, WI

My Future, Our Nation

As I consider my future worth
The stress and constant questions are at a max girth

As I pack my bag
What and who do I take?
Do I pack until the bag breaks?
Do I stuff until I reach closure?
Or just pack light to save composure
Do I take the people who benefit me?
Or drag along bums around my grand prix?

I lived around the saying "family first"
But if my mother asks me one more question about future, I'll burst

So the questions resume, what and who do I take?
Just keep the past?
Which seems to never make my happiness last

Actually, do I even pack for my future? Or just start clean?
Maybe, me, myself and I is the best team

I'm simply nineteen years old and I am fed up being forced into decision
My whole life's ahead and the only way to succeed is with precision

So why try to control the future generation?
Leave it up to us, who knows we might change the nation

Daniel Buser
New Milford, CT

Oprah Oprah

Oprah, Oprah, what a great person you are!
You're like a moonbeam shining through a star.
You're inspiring and thoughtful in stories you share.
Give insight to people whose tragedies they bear.

You've given away gifts that blow one's mind,
Like cars, trips; that is so sublime.
You bring unknown talent and make them a star.
Oprah, people love you; they come from near and far.

I love your enthusiasm, love your style.
When I watch your show you make me smile.
Twenty-five years have come and gone.
Now, you can sing your last swan song.

But Oprah, Oprah, I'll always remember you.
You'll always be successful in whatever you do.
Some day you might even want to go to Mars,
(And if you do)
Your moonbeam will still be shining through the stars!

Elaine Freeman
Sacramento, CA

Decorations

I love my decorations
when Halloween is
near.
The skeleton is hanging from
the chandelier.
The witch is on the door
and the cat is on the floor
and ghosts and goblins are
floating door to door.
Although they are not real
I love them just the same
for when I put them
all away I call them all
by name.

Terry Albers
Dardenne Prairie, MO

To Those Who Fear Me

To those who fear me:
Throw me into the water to see if
I'll drown or you can try to burn me at
the stake, but I won't give up without a
fight. Perhaps you'd like it best if I didn't
conjure and play with magic or maybe
it's because I can't wrinkle and wither away
with age. But mark my words! You're
fate is in the palm of your hands. Scram
and cry, you have no one to blame but
yourself. Your beauty shall be shattered
and hung, your flesh stripped away from
your bones. I'll keep your precious
hearts but sell your
souls to the devil down below.

Teia Horton
Athens, MI

Always with You

Know that I am fine, within the daylight of my darkness unknown to you.
Know how much I shine, and am at peace within
the darkness of your daylight, no longer mine.
Know that I love you now, and even more than all of our befores gone by.
Know that I am here, yet there is your everywhere!
See me in your own heart's eye, with no longer a sigh, or the question "why?"
Remember my life, swift in passing is now so wonderfully ever-lasting!
I am free to live happily 'neath the sun of God's green divide.
Yes, the center of your world is at rest completely,
living serenely within His love divine.
And though you may miss me, to touch and to hold,
know that I'm with thee, 'til eternity unfolds.
Just remember the love between us and He,
and that one day again, together we'll be.
But for now my beloved, I'll say good-night,
as I clasp the candle of your spirit light.
For when your journey begins anew,
you'll know my love is
always with you.

Tricia Downey
Hamilton, ON

It gives me inner peace and pleasure to share my humble perspective in a manner by which the numerously sad souls of our day can identify. I wrote "Always with You" from the point of view that we, all of us, do pass on, leaving those whom we love behind. For this respect, the poem is written from the perspective of the one who has passed, reminding us that their abiding love and spirit lives on, extending comfort as we move forward, toward the ultimate reunion in the knowledge that we, indeed, are the better and the richer for having been loved!

The Lover

Among alfalfa fields affable he slides
with his blizzard hands plays
mussing the green Amates tree foliage
the ochres cornfields lie down
to the ineffable slightest touch of his caresses

He? He fiddles play with the moist herb
and in an harmonic swaying of baleful waves
engenders hope and promises life

But I… I know him!
That devastating charm
is like cobs cumulus
threshed by the wind
and heartless snatches away
bitter tears
rending the sky

Yessica Rodriguez
Beaverton, OR

Artemis

Goddess of the hunt, slayer in the wood
My pack accompany me
As do arrow and hood

Seeking refuge from the men, who I so yearn for
They will die by my sword
—I shan't be their whore

For feathered creatures and smiling fangs,
My soul is given over
Mortals have no place in my heart, only an occasional lover

Beware to him, who finds his way close
At first a rapturous rumble,
—Then I become morose

So off goes his head!
And once again,
Diana returns to her empty bed

Bloodied not bereaved, with a dispassionate stare
I now resume my guard
Ethereal winds, whispering through my hair

The hawk be my wings, and wolf prevent my freeze
Forever I am alone,
Hidden among the trees

Good night Moon Goddess
My friend, not a foe
You live inside me, yet already know

Diana Hunt
Santa Fe, NM

Everything Happens for a Reason

I don't know where to start, I don't know where to begin,
because sometimes I feel hollow inside and within.

I've been fighting against this monster inside me, and
I quite can't find the key to see the light in the deep blue sea.

Doing things out of frustration, smiling but close to tearing up.
For the first time I realized, this is making me crazy but I never give up.

I always have hope no matter what. I know there are hard times,
but I lift up my head and climb the tree to see the light that I seek.

I resist, I fight, I battle through the rough, but I know in my
heart the stars come through when there is no moon out.

I went through it all, I've been through worse,
I don't need anything but to just break this curse.

Stephanie Caldero
West Hartford, CT

My name is Stephanie Caldero. I am sixteen years old and 2014 was the worst year of my life. I had knee surgery in April and recovery was brutal. But the worst part of the year wasn't that; I spent six weeks in the Institute of Living, being diagnosed with anxiety, depression, extreme mood changes, and thought disorder. Life has its ups and downs, but you always have to have hope. There are millions of boys and girls suffering and I want to let them know, they are not alone. Life is a story and this is my journey.

Nature's Voice

Nature's always speaking to me,
Showing me its world,
It whispers to me lightly,
Inspiring my soul.

Everything's connected,
It says to me all the time,
And even if we leave a place,
In front is our behind.

Nothing really leaves us,
For everything's the same,
And in this tiny seashell,
This all can be explained.

The mountains, are somewhere by us,
The sea, is nowhere near,
Our life, is always with us,
And yet all of it is here.

Kristen Vargas
Highlands Ranch, CO

I created a poetry club with my best friend, Monika Marsh. We got seashells and wrote about what we saw. I saw a shell from the ocean with swirls in shapes of mountains. I believe we can learn a lot from nature, as it connects all forms of life. The world is big, but everything in it is a part of one strong unit. Even though oceans and mountains aren't a few steps away, they're still here and affect us. Life is all around, near and far, and big or small it all plays a role, found in nature's voice.

Spiteful Insidious Goddess

An angry heartbroken angel fallen from the glory of grace.
A beautifully pure, and genuine soul turned hostile,
violently provoked into the darkness by the many cruel,
ungrateful, bastards that took her power, and bottomless love
for granted.
The most innocent, passionate being hurt so severely and
intensely, that it changed her,
morphed her into an aggressive, spiteful insidious goddess.
She is no longer a minion of the good side,
no longer a messenger for god.
She has been dealing with the corruption and abuse for a
much too long eternity, and it has finally broken her,
taken her over, possessing her with such resentment
and fury, that she is no longer willing or able to feel
even the slightest tinge of pain or fear,
regret or remorse;
her joy, hope, and once unconditional love for everyone
and everything, was stolen from her.
The only emotion that the demons spared her is
unquenchable rage.
Her spirit dying along with her faith,
her heart withering so everly, irretrievably,
far, far away.

Olivia Trudeau
Milwaukee, WI

I have been writing poetry since I was twelve and it has become the most important part of my life. I write to express my emotions and the events happening in my life. I wrote "Spiteful Insidious Goddess" shortly after my mother passed away from cancer. I discovered she was sick when I was sixteen, and I dropped out of school to take care of her. The experience was dreadful but it made me who I am today. This poem is dedicated to Andrea Trudeau. Rest in peace, Mom, I love you.

Wind and Flame

like a *whisper*
you were gone from my life
a soft *breeze*
flowing
tumbling around as
if on *clouds*
I can feel
your *strength*
resonating
in my bones
flowing
filling my limbs
with *fire*
as if they were hot
coals, breathing
in the night
like a *whisper*
you were gone from my life
you kept all that I had
you never returned

Paige Smith
Spearfish, SD

Cancer Is a Journey

The word "cancer" tears your heart out, it takes your breath away
Your future is uncertain, and you're challenged day by day.
Cancer has no boundaries, when it comes to strife and pain
It can cause turmoil and suffering, as you learn to dance in the rain.

You have a brand new journey, it matters not about the past
Writing future chapters, with family friends and cast.
The doctors and the nurses... are there to help you mend
They walk with you through storms, and help you calm the winds.

Stay positive in all areas, don't bring negative words to life
Your thoughts and words are crucial, they choose your day or night.
Your journey will have detours, the road ahead is curvy
Go by faith and not by sight, don't waste your time with worry.

Laughter really is the best medicine, there's nothing like a smile
It warms the heart and lightens the load as you go that extra mile.
Finding humor isn't easy, sometimes you have to dig real deep
Watch funny movies, laugh out loud, and hug God before you sleep.

God is the one who's in control, he will see you through
Put your faith and trust in him, and let Jesus guide you too.
Step through each door with courage, don't fret about tomorrow
Make the most of today—be sure you pray—and God will ease your sorrow.

Teresa Abbott
Aberdeen, OH

I recently discovered my passion for writing after my battle with cancer. Once I began, the words just started falling from my heart. I especially love to personalize stories into poems. Doing this touches my heart, as I watch emotions unfold on the face of those recipients. My illness inspired me to write "Cancer Is a Journey" in hopes that it will give strength and courage to those traveling that same road. I am now writing a book about my journey in hopes that it too will be an inspiration.

On Going Home

I woke to a black void
Alone among fifty
Times one thousand feet
Chilled
Discomforted
Disoriented

My watch hands were vertical
I, horizontal
It was no time
I was between seconds

The metal womb
Sped above a watery grave
A no-man's land
That infinitesimal moment
Between turning back
And the point of no return.

No choice
The hands moved

But I had a window on the world
And I saw it
That celestial crucifix
In the southern sky

I was going home!

Fay Brett
Naples, FL

Untitled

There is a majesty about my room
It's quite complete

Sky and sea and hills are under roof
and people of all shapes and sizes

The wild and domestic dwell within
weaning babies, adding colors, adding sent

Listen close, the cricket chirps, the spigot drips
the tree is rustled by the wind
it's quite complete

There is a majesty about my room
you have a key, you are invited in

Sheldon Wallerstein
Palm Beach Gardens, FL

My Real Christmas

Faith, love and family
Gold, frankincense and myrrh
Three wise men
Holy blessed Trinity
Holy Spirit, Jesus and God

Mary, Joseph and Jesus
Love, faith and family
Trust, hope and spirit

Holly, wreath, bells
Eggnog, pumpkin pie, turkey / ham
Friends, family, parties
Mistletoe, tree, angels

Children laughing and
Singing, people dancing
And bells ringing

This is what Christmas
Truly means to me, and
Why Jesus is the reason
For this holiday season

Barbara Roberts
Rock Hill, SC

I grew up in South Dakota. At age eighteen I joined the Navy and served three years. I married a sailor. We divorced twenty-seven years later. I always liked to write and draw and do crafts. I have drawn all kinds of pictures for friends and family. Then I started designing and making cards for all occasions, sometimes with poems in them. I currently work as a certified nursing assistant and have been since 1996. I love people, my job, drawing, writing, and my husband of nine years. I have written short stories and poems.

Life

Fault no one for your place in life.
  Not your friends, enemies, husband or wife.
For who you are, or who you will someday be,
  Is no one else's responsibility.

It's always easier to put the blame,
  On someone else for a dying flame.
But most that finally do succeed,
  Do so to satisfy an inner need.

Joe E. Buczek
Surfside Beach, SC

Parched Land

Drip, drip, drip.
Slowly the tear drops slide down the face of the earth,
Quenching the thirst of the ever so patient dryads.
Streaming veins paint the barren skin of the ground
With moisture and bringing life to whatever it touches.
Then,
The heavenly realms open revealing
The scorching sun drying everything and shining on anything
And God's covenant enchants the sky
With streaks of beautiful color.

Jonathan Ovidiu Olar
Boca Raton, FL

The Defining Driver

What drives me?
What is this feeling?
The desire…
The passion…
Overwhelming, yes
Electrifying, yes
Defining, I do not know, others say
Ripping and tearing me apart
Overpowering, sometimes against my will
Driven hard, very hard… to this unfathomable point
Weakening me in their eyes
Sad or elated once spent
Do I really have a choice… Do you?
Who am I?
Are we all such, same… yes
Except for the *others*

Harold Henderson
Grand Bay, AL

December

Winter is now here.
Lights are bright and colorful.
The season to give.

Minnie Chau
Hillsboro, OR

Solitude

Oh the joy of solitude, one does not realize
until his world is filled with noise
and constant peering eyes.
I like to walk through woodlands
deep and let my mind run free
or sit down to meditate beneath
an old oak tree.
I like to feel cool grass beneath
my back and watch the clouds
roll by:
and wonder what life is all
about and why we have to die.

Johnny Hickey
Chattanooga, TN

Approach to Liberty

Can you see the image of that empty space
Dare to dream what belongs in its place
Clean white socks without any holes
Out with friends on long afternoon strolls
Take a moment and visualize
With your determinations, this dream will materialize
Wherever you go, you make a contribution
No matter if you're out there or in an institution
Crimes are not always punished on logical terms deserved
But in the end, justice will always be served
And rewards are dealt the very same hand
That comes directly from the highest command
It's the effect that your actions generate
That will become anything you would like to create
Get a ledger, keep a score
If you win, you'll find what you've been looking for

Patricia Teofilo
Mobile, AL

A Royal Plea

Oh Lily, you who won't wear pants.
The one who loves to be dressed in elegance,
edged with spoken soft words of romance.

You are my source of joy,
one of the world's greatest treasures.
Through you I find, my divine pleasure.
Your power is amazing, your will fierce.
A gloomy day, your sweetness will pierce.

You are pushy, particular—
you don't like what I wear.
You want everything quite fair,
from my toes to my hair.

Oh, I am sorry to be a spoilsport,
hiding you in disguise, slumming out of the court.
You are a queen, a passionate one,
one who likes resting, playing—lying about in the sun.
If only I could step back, your will would be done.

For now, you want to be left alone,
no kings or princes in this courtly home.
Only tempting morsels like mirth, skirts—the scent of the earth,
feed your being beyond words,
revealing to me, your glorious worth.

Suzanne Odland
Wheaton, IL

In poetry, I hear the rhythm of life. Every beat touches the hidden parts of my underused heart, unleashing a joy my mind has never known and one my soul hoped I would someday find. "A Royal Plea" tells the story of an inner queen, tired of a hectic week spent checking off tasks in an old pair of jeans. May you revel in her rebellion.

A Crow's Caw

Entrust the crow and life will never be your own
because lies fill his beak and a new truth is known.
You still hold your secrets, but they don't even measure
to the crow's hurtful tales he sees as his treasure.
The value you place on your word is on loan
to the parasitic leech who now steals your throne.
In untruths he prospers and gives himself pleasure
as you lick your wounds and survive at his leisure.
His threats don't allow you to utter a moan
for fear of his caw that you may never atone.
The cruelty he cries is so strong and so sure
assuring the destruction of truth and what's pure.
A crow's evil caw should send chills to the bone
so always strike first, but aim well with your stone.

Tom Middleton
Germantown, TN

Silence

Listen to the...
Silence
The golden edge of spectrum,
Listen to the...
Silence
The heartbeat quietly in tune?
A steady and constant beat stream
A constancy of mean.

Listen to the...
Silence
A quiet unnerving scene.
Listen to the ...
Silence
A regeneration rebound?
I cannot stand the...
Silence
A peace not really found.
Listen to all the...
Silence
The action does not compound.
Listen to the...
Silence
Nary a distant sound!

Betty Perry
Rockwell, TX

To My Family

It's almost time to say good-bye
as Mother Time is counting down
the final days here on this earth
which we cannot stop or turn around

I think about the years gone by
how swiftly time has passed
the twilight zone is very near
almost within one's grasp

I remember well those childhood days
that were so long ago
when memories were being made
like a potter daily molding clay

But as the years have come and gone
my thoughts go back again
to all the times both good and bad
and think what might have been

And so I hope when I depart
that I will have left behind
some good and happy memories
that will stay forever in your mind

I love you all so very much
my great big family
keep Jesus always in your hearts
'til we meet again in eternity

Ruth Stricker
Siloam Springs, AR

Season's Turnaround

Reasons abound for season's turnaround
Morning light, misty and bright
Gentle breeze, soft and light
Stream gently through leafless branch
Dewdrops ablaze in morning sun
Resemble glittering lights of Christmas bright
Snow in the glade resting in shade
Holly berries delight
With sight of sun's perfect light
Red and gold dance on backdrop of green and white
Winter's solstice not far behind
Trees barren of leaves prepare for winter's rest
An abandoned nest, evidence of new life
A blanket of snow on frozen ground,
Shelter spring bulb, await season's turnaround

Dennis Superczynski
Knoxville, TN

Cream Puffs and Cannolis

Never really trusted my skinny friends
They could eat and were always slim

Am I paying for some past life karma
Did I call someone *fat*
If so God, I'm so sorry for that

My closet is full of every size
I shop for clothes to help me disguise
These voluptuous hips, and bulging thighs

I rip out the Chubby Chick label
God forbid someone should see

Move over tight fitting jeans
Only stretch waistbands for me
I don't know about you, but, I like to breathe

God my life was not meant to be like this
I retain water faster than a sinking ship

Please God, send me a sign, something to brighten my day

Oh look! A coupon for an
All you can eat buffet!

Carol Macari
Charlotte, NC

Waiting

Before you left, we walked and talked
 A lot of reminisce.
We had a picnic on the ground
 And parted with a kiss.

The maple, elm and oak were dressed
 In shades of red and brown.
You mentioned you'd be back before
 The snow came swirling down.

Last month the maple lost its leaves
 In storm of wind and rain.
The elm soon followed with leaves
 That filled the lane.

It seems so long that you've been gone,
 So long you've been away.
I watched the oak with anxious eye.
 The last leaf fell today.

Viola Sagebiel
Kansas City, MO

Love's Elusiveness

Like a warm summer breeze
Gently ripples through the trees,
Feelings silently and calmly starts
Imbuing and capturing our hearts

From where they come we don't know
But feelings often continue to grow,
Then subtle as they appear
Feelings just up and disappear

We wonder where those feelings went
And how they all got spent,
Guess life happens that way
Feelings are never meant to stay

Still when life treats us unkind
And joy is so hard to find,
We can recall that time
When love was yours and mine

Jerry Randolph
Daphne, AL

Jesus Is Love and Peace and Unity

Together we can find, peace through grace,
Hope through happiness,
Jesus through the mines of our souls,
And unity through togetherness only, if you are willing to cope.
Only if you believe, you can achieve.

Twanda Stewart
Rock Hill, SC

What Is a Son?

A son is a blessing forthright and true,
A son is God's reflection upon you.
A son is the one whom holy truths you bestow,
A son is the one in which you watch grace grow.
A son is the one in which all your hopes come true,
A son is the one in which the reflection is greater than you.
A son is the one in whom you place your heart's desire,
A son is the one in by which righteous faith aspires.
A son is the one in whom you hope his dreams come true,
A son is the one who honors by giving God all that is due.
A son is the one in all he perseveres,
A son is the one in all walks God he most reveres.

Daniel Glen Baker
Houston, TX

Break Me

Feeling is precious,
Knowing what to feel all the more,
Those who've the advantage,
Have never had to ignore.

Unbearable, that I can't deny,
All predictability gone,
Something between the lie,
It can never be undone.

Tomorrow may be bright,
Forever might never come,
Whatever's in my sights,
Hold fast to summer's hum.

Know you're constant,
Breathe your light,
Feel not nothing,
But the acknowledgement of night.

Alexandra Lacey
Camarillo, CA

Cap'n Jon

Ah, the wharf of a sailor's tale
How deep and blithe is she
Entranced how he came by the sail
Wrought into the man he be
Sojourn abroad as the wind
For this, I care not
His lifestyle, evanescent
Here with me, he's caught
Grand with magnificence
Where he has been
Spare the grandiloquence
He is my friend
We sit here, drinking
Just whiskey
Colloquial-ing
Pine the sea
Simple fondness
For life
With him, I'm bless'd
In rife
In fervor
We
In grandeur
Sea

Christopher Cleland
Glendale, AZ

While I am mainly a songwriter, I chose to take a moment to commemorate one of my best friends, Jonathan, a member of the US Coast Guard, through my poem "Cap'n Jon." Jonathan is an incredible man who deserves to tell grandiose "sailor's tales," but his humility vastly supercedes most of his other qualities. He has no air of superiority or bombastic ostentatiousness, though he deserves and has every right to it! Thank you for taking the time to read it. I hope it reminds you of someone in your own life. We are all friends of legends.

What Is the Mind of Messiah

You appealed to me in my wilderness
Liberated my salvation because of it
It was ordained before time in my purposes
I stood, I fell, now rise on level surfaces

It is you, God, in me, God

Who teaches and loves, preaches and shoves
To get my attention without apprehension
There's no reservation about these relations

With me, God

You see the things of my past, nullify things that don't last
Eternity has started so I live life whole-hearted
Demanding to see what's before me, crying out on bended knee
Expectantly

It is you, God, in me, God

Torah that breathes life into the bones of insurrection
Grace that fills in the gaps of my imperfections
Devouring the bread of life that sustains me
While diving into the absoluteness of things unseen

It is you, God, in me, God

What is the mind of Messiah?
A secret transformation, I shall not hide it
Forbearers of righteousness denied it
Generations are being drawn to abide in it

Traci E. Adams
Honolulu, HI

Courage

Is there courage hiding somewhere
inside of me tonight?
For, if there is, I need you now
before dawn's early light
I need to know that I can cope
with whatever comes my way,
optimistic and untroubled
at the start of the new day
I've heard it said "that I must hide
if my feelings are forlorn,"
for people admire winners
"and the losers they will scorn"
Tonight I'm needing courage, for grey
clouds surround my heart,
I'm feeling like I'm all alone, and
just may fall apart
I'm trying to adjust my sails
through peace and meditation,
hoping my direction, becomes a
peaceful destination

Gail Cochrane
Poway, CA

Harvest Moon

Just a sliver at first,
then a half moon,
peeks out from
behind the mountain.
Soon the whole moon,
a perfectly formed orb
the color of fresh cream,
hangs over Mount Jumbo
like a sentinel at post
ready to protect and defend
the inhabitants of the city below.

Moonlight floods
even the darkest ravine
on this mid-September evening,
causing the soon-to-be leafless trees
to shimmer and sway in the breeze.
Hours later the moon
glows even brighter,
like a giant orange
suspended by invisible thread
in the crisp night sky,
as hard working residents
slumber on, oblivious
to the beauty of this splendid sight.

Sherry Knight Rossiter
Missoula, MT

The Photo Album

The photo album, it puts in place puzzle pieces of our life
Putting together thoughtfully, our times of joy and strife
Some black and white, some color bright, some scenes
we can't recall
But, it is documented proof of our world when were small
We look each time with eyes renewed at relatives and friends
We find little things we'd overlooked caught by the
camera lens
It is to us a treasure chest
The first thing packed in a time of stress
It is a thing we can't replace
A look, a smile, a loving face of someone who has
left our sight
Coming back once more to hold on tight
To us they haven't left at all as our mind goes
back and we recall
Clearly now like it was yesterday, we reenact
our private play
We look upon our times of cheer and count the
ones who are still here
We see family we've added on to help ease the pain
of those who've gone
So this is what I think each time I open it to see
The past, the present, they all complete the
puzzle piece that's me

Linda Feeley
Spring Hill, FL

In Loving Memory Of

You are my dad
When you took my mom's hand in marriage
you took all of us too
 You are my dad
You were there when I needed a shoulder
to cry on, when a boyfriend broke up
with me
 You are my dad
You were there to get onto me when I
messed up, it was a lot
 You are my dad
You were there to see the birth of my
children and watch them grow
 You are my dad
You were there to watch my children
become young adults
 You are my dad
 Continue to watch over us from heaven
and know that everyday I will think
of you and see you in my children
as they start families of their own
 You are my dad
You will always be the rock that I
leaned on
 You will always be my father

Vonda Newall
Colcord, OK

Lament

The moon was shining brightly
As I walked about last night
I looked up and tried to see you
But you're hidden from my sight

I closed my eyes and whispered
Your name, your name
But all I heard was silence
And blame and shame

I should have been there with you
When you took your final breath
I should have sat beside you
When you closed your eyes in death

You knew that I was coming
That I was on my way
Oh, just a few more minutes
I had so much to say

Please forgive me, Mother
I'm trying to atone
For soon my time is coming
And I will die alone

Then we'll be together
For all eternity
You and me and Daddy
And Pop and Sweet Momee

Patsy Wiggins
Chattanooga, TN

Twilight Fading

...have to rush
these trembling words
my fingers unshaking brush.
Can't even see the page
alleviated is my rage
on a day so very sweet
surely the kindest dream to meet.
104, smiling faces, the glory
I can call all my own
With all I want as a result
to save you, from being alone.
Goddesses whisper my name
as I play willing in their game.
Yet, the only glory I long to see
is you, you, right next to me.
Please, by the end of the night, that
against now I race,
please, please, embrace my soul
that after you, only you, with
weary wings and bleeding feet, does chase...

Savannah Dillashaw
Port Orange, FL

I've Got Cancer, but It Doesn't Have Me

I've got cancer, that terrible "C,"
It's got my body, but it doesn't have me.
It's taken residence up in my colon,
It's in my nodes, my liver's swollen.
I have a portal, my body's tapped,
I'm treated with chemo, my energy's zapped.
My hair is falling, I cannot sleep,
And in the darkness, I worry… weep.

Then I remember this horrible "C"
Is just an illness, it's not me.
For I was born of immigrant stock
From struggles and fears I shall not balk.
I am a sister, a friend, a mother, a wife,
An artist, a gardener with a zest for this life.
I'm a PT, a neighbor, and very gregarious.
I'm social and personable and often hilarious.

I am Tish, Patricia D.
I've got cancer, but it doesn't have me.

Anne M. Moreland
Cape Girardeau, MO

Angels

Angels they are everywhere if only we could see
The beauty of their presence surrounding you and me.

Ask and angels will appear to help us when we call
They will pick us up again and bless us when we fall.

Do not be in fear, they come here to assist
They're messengers to love and heal, how can we resist?

The brightness of their aura, their massive strength of wings.
Angels lift us up to heaven to be with God our king.

When our days come to an end and our life unfolds,
All our deeds kept in a book will now be read and told.

You see the angels do record everything we've done,
So we can stand before our Lord to account for webs we've spun.

Isabel Lucas
Calabash, NC

I was inspired to write this poem by my wonderful Parkinson's support group leader, Beverly. I have had visits by beautiful angels three times in my life. This is why I chose "Angels" as my title.

My Love for You

The ocean,
Is like a reflection,
Of my love for you.

It's like each wave,
That beats upon the shore.

My heart,
Thumping, beating,
Vigorously for you.

As I stare into the ocean,
I see a reflection,
Of me to you.

What calm, what peace,
What love, I feel for you.

My love for you,
Surpasses the brightness of the sun,
As it glimmers upon the ocean,
It brings a glow,
That can never be extinguished.

Now I see clearly,
As I look upon the ocean waves,
My love for you is as my heartbeat,
Which beats vehemently each day for you.

As the ocean waves,
Rolls to shore,
My love for you,
Will never cease.

Gailyn Saahir
Pembroke Pines, FL

Dementia

Where are my mother's words?
Where are her thoughts… gone.
I look at her
And she is not there.
I talk to her
And an absent sight
Is the only response.
I hold her hand.
I hold her tight
To let her know
That no matter what
She will always be
Deep in my heart.

Maria Isaza
Smithfield, NC

Maria Isaza was born in Medellin, Colombia, in 1956. She studied modern languages at Universidad Pontificia Bolivariana. She began teaching, got married and had three daughters. In 2000, she divorced and lost her youngest child. In 2008, she was hired to teach English in North Carolina. She married in 2010. Her passions are teaching, writing and knitting. She is convinced that "life gives you back what you give to life."

Clutching My Pearls

Trying to protect the lining of my inner soul. The lining like intestines from a pig all balled up ready for a stew you want to season. The canker worms have eaten away what must be restored. The lining is thin and has been stretched out by the lies, the deception, by time. I am now realizing that my life is important. All the years that have passed have torn at my lining. Leaving the light flickering. Feeling unfulfilled, lonely, wanting more than what has been given to me. I am wanting to devour all that remains of me, because I am not available for the pain anymore. I am not available for the dust of my history. I am not available for the roots of my existence to be snatched by what others have plotted to plow. My story is rich yet my foremothers have shown me different. They didn't wait around for me to grow, they set the good soil to the side and fertilized and tried to murder my being with the darkness of their handicaps. They killed her soul and passed the remnants of the recipe down in the lining of my core. Sopped it with uncooked dough because they did not want me to rise. You tried to stop the seed from growing in her one time, you tried to stop the seed from growing in her four times. Now those seeds have been planted in dark red bone soil pushing from beneath the grave.

Diane Washington
Maderia Beach, FL

I am the daughter of Mary Alice Washington. I am a native New Yorker. I am a motivational speaker. I am a poet. I am a first lady. I am Rev. Greg Jones's wife. I am the mother of Shawana, Simone and Sadie. I am the grandmother of Lenoxx and Aires. I am the founder of Womanly Wisdom Ministries, which allows me to travel and speak to women of various afflictions who have been shackled and handcuffed to traditional strongholds of their self esteem. I am the woman who has come from a long line of secret genesis. I am the woman with the amazing revelation.

Time

Time is something, when we're born
We never really think of,

But time is swiftly, moving on
Incredible to think on

When we were adults we think
About many different matters

Time is not one of them
That really seems to matter

When we are old, we think about
The things when we were young

The time we spent in growing up
Of wasting time and loving

But time goes on, and then we die
But have we contemplated

On the time, the precious time
We have just invaded

"Memo"
Not really—unless we love
memories

Make them the best we can

Nancy Jensen
Lund, NV

His Claim

I painted Heaven and Earth
from beyond the sky.
I came down from Heaven
for man
to die.

I forgive and forget.
I heal sin and regret.
I pour grace and mercy.
I fill all the thirsty.

I turned water into wine
to prove I'm divine.
What more do you need?
I'm yours.
You're mine.

Jordon Colombo
Rancho Santa Margarita, CA

I'm Taking Care of You

Should I fall asleep to awake no more—
I know I'll land on that "golden shore,"
anxious to pass through that "golden door,"
anxious to see loved ones who've gone before.

Some days discouragement creeps in to overtake,
"Down in the dumps," a sad disposition does make.
Perhaps if the sun rises, brilliantly shining—
my outlook will improve, interrupting my whining!

With my head on my pillow, I can only look up,
reminding me God's there, still "filling my cup."
That's all I need my mood to change—
shattering my blues, my outlook to rearrange.

That still small voice once more had come through:
"Jan, I'm taking care of you."
What more could I ask, from my "best friend,"
walking beside me to the very end!

How often before, I have heard His voice,
helping solve life's problems or showing a better choice!
Thank you Lord, for "umpteen" times You've come through
with 'Jan,' I'm taking care of you."

Janet Gosney
Clearwater, FL

Ghost Street

I was on my way home from work, it wasn't quite dark yet. The traffic was heavy as usual or for lack of a better word congested. I had to stop at Walmart, before I turned into the parking lot. I had a sudden thought or should I say a flash back. I was thinking about all the people including my parents, my brothers who have either driven, walked or at least made this thoroughfare, better known as I-65 service road, a familiar hang out spot or perhaps it was someone's way home or just got to go to Walmart place. The point I am getting at is a lot of those people are no longer a part of this earthly realm. And then I took that memory a step further, wouldn't it be nice to have had a hidden camera to see all those happy as they looked… then faces. I think that would be awesome, if we could go back in time to capture those images.

Or look through the lens of life moments frozen in time, memories reflections of the way it was from the expressions of timeless faces that once crowded the streets, which will only be part of a very special place… will always be with us locked in time in which I call Ghost Street.

Cynthia R. Poe
Mobile, AL

Untitled

Only broken vessels can
be mended, only broken
hearts can be forgiven.
Thank you Lord for the
brokenness that I feel.
Cleanse my soul and do
your will. I've been on
the mountaintop, and
I've been in the valley
too. But Lord, when
I'm broken, that's when
I'm nearest you. When
all seems to be lost, and
there's nothing left to
gain, that's when He
reaches down and heals
our deepest pain.

Bobby Griffin
Meridian, MS

A Dream

Here I am all alone
Not away
Nowhere to call my home
I'm inside out
I'm upside down
I'm so dizzy and turned around
I'm falling up
I'm falling down
I'm in another part of town
I'm just not sure
Where I could beam
Eureka, I'm in a dream

Karen Neubauer
Fulton, MO

I come from a family of five. My mom and dad have passed away. I only have contact with one of my sisters. Her name is Nancy. What inspired my poem was the way I feel at times. I just called it "A Dream." That's all I really have to say. My mom and dad's names were Darell and Bonnie. My sisters are Nancy, Bev, Misty, and Jana.

Trekie's Eyes

Trekie, soft, cuddly, squirming ball of fur.
Tail wagging, she looks up at me
Eyes shining with the reflection of God's unconditional love.

Trekie, watching, patiently waiting by the window for my return,
Greets me at the door.
Tail wagging, she looks up at me
Eyes shining with the reflection of God's unconditional love.

Trekie, today, no longer able to watch,
Still waiting patiently by the window for my return,
Greets me at the door.
Tail wagging, looks up at me with her sight-dimmed eyes
Still shining with the reflection of God's unconditional love.

Kathleen A. Esser
Wendell, NC

War Is Hell

I turn around.
Another buddy fell.
In these clothes, it's hard to tell.
Must be quiet, but I want to yell.
In a little while
I may rest a spell.
Want to go home, take my place
Need to kiss my baby's face,
Sing songs about God's grace.
What I'd give for a quiet place.
Another time we'll be face to face.
So long pal of mine
My number's up
It's my time.

Poet L. A. Wright
Pinellas Park, FL

The Colors in My Blanket

Here I am under my blanket.
So warm and beautiful.
It is simple and drapes over my bed,
For it was made with love.
My mom made my blanket.
She made it with her own beautiful hands.
I will treasure this.
She had no sewing machine,
But she had to sew by hand.
I watched her day and night.
My Mom told me stories so long ago.
For I sat and listened.
I enjoyed spending time with her
Because she knew what colors to match.
Her hands were worn.
She did not care, for she knew I needed a blanket.
Winter was coming soon.
I adored my mom for making my blanket.
My eyes grew bigger for I knew it would be done.
I came home from school.
There was my surprise on my bed.
I turned around and gave her a hug.
She knew I loved my colored blanket.
I felt safe under my blanket.
My blanket is a treasure from my mom.
My mom made it with her beautiful hands.

Pauline Byrnes
Mineral Point, WI

The inspiration for my poem is a person who was very special to me, my mom. When I was young and as winter was approaching, my mom decided that I needed a blanket. She had amazing taste when it came to matching up colors and used those skills to make me a blanket of my very own. It was so beautiful and so well crafted that I still have it today, even though she passed away many years ago. With that in mind, I wanted to do this poem to pay tribute to Mom.

The Absence of Light

My heart has turned cold and hard,
Too much of reality does this to you.
Hands shaking, adrenaline pumping, and the craving for destruction
Flows through my veins.
Emptiness is something I have become accustomed to.
Eventually the aches of tortured past finally let go
And I am free.
But this is an unknown feeling,
To be lost in the autumn leaves and have nothing else to fall back on
Except for distant hopes of a possible future.
A permanent corruption lingers in my thoughts
And anger motivates my actions
Because nothing else matters
When your soul is lost in darkness.

Courtney Malinowski
Worth, IL

Untitled

I'm a slave to my own causes
I'm the king of dependent clauses
Life is too simple, thanks Tristan
Life is full of God, thanks Christian

A hotel, quivering in the embrace of tectonic plates
Tsunami city: a diagnosis of the world's aches

Help me, I'm trapped in time
Entropy's claws gracefully hold mine

What?
You're leaving?

I can't follow my thoughts
Once it gets stressful it's lost
It sinks down into the abyss of my mind

I can't die yet, I haven't finished my work
My pride, my joy, the only reason I lurk
Around this Earth, just a constructive interference
Quantum qualities in between some decoherence

Fuck off, Descartes

Daniel Guilliams
Raleigh, NC

Some Days

There are days she hates the sadness.
Days it creeps under eyelids, unaware of its presence
until morning alarms scream
and eyelids are stuck shut, hurting to open, hurting to see.
Days when it claws,
talons deep into muscles and tendons and bones,
nesting in her brain and snipping neurons
so smiles touch lips, never eyes.
It is clinical. It is deep.
It is unpredictable,
this sadness.

But there are days,
entire days, when she loves the sadness.
Days when words electrify her tongue and burst
into song. Days her eyes shine, and love,
and see everything in vibrant living color.
On these days she celebrates the sadness,
twirling it around her head, throwing it into the air,
popping into confetti, trapping in hair, gathering at feet.
She revels the world of echoed, embracing laughter.
Each day is new. Each day is alive.
Some days hurt. Most do not.
The days now dance, and she dances with them,
always thanking sadness
for allowing her to feel joy.

Erin Mary Beirne
Santa Ana, CA

Kaleidoscope Eyes

Kaleidoscope eyes,
falling to rise,
the color wheel,
a changing of tides,
blink too fast it'll disappear,
replaced with something new,
ignorance retaliates with fear,
Kaleidoscope eyes,
falling to rise,
the color wheel,
a changing of tides,
never empty,
always endearing,
charmed in,
by change of appearance,
Yes,
things will hide,
in your kaleidoscope eyes,
which fall to rise,
with a color wheel,
and a changing of tides,
...your kaleidoscope eyes.

Emilia Petty
Dover, DE

Emilia Petty is a fourteen-year-old artist from Dover, Delaware. She loves to draw using colored pencils, markers and oil pastels. She also loves to sculpt with polymer clay. She revels in photography and finds inspiration in the shapes and colors of nature. She also relaxes by doing Zentangle art. She is currently working on an art entry of decorated light bulbs for the state fair.

Home but Not Returned

Sent to the boot camp at such a young age
Faced with Drill Instructors filled with rage.
Graduate camp with the highest amount of pride.
Now headed to Afghanistan awaiting a very long ride.

Bullets fly past the men's heads with no known destination
They reconsider their choice to defend their nation.
Caught under fire, the ones hit just lie and moan.
All this means is that their location is known.

The adrenaline rush of death knocking on their front door.
The thrill of this experience, there is nothing more.
The attackers' luck of staying alive, has surly slid.
They check the dead bodies, to find a little kid.

Returning home for the Fourth of July is the best news to hear.
The things the men have gone through, only one thing is feared:
Hiding from fireworks to avoid the memories,
Of the many attacks, brought to them by their enemies.

For the rest of their lives, remembering the lives they've seen pass.
Their many brothers falling in a pile of brass.
The training protects these soldiers from damage from any kind.
But no one can see what goes on in their mind.

Their live bodies may come home, away from the field,
But their memories from their days overseas, forever concealed.

Tyrone Jeronimo
Stamford, CT

Growing up, I've always looked at our nation's military with respect. I've also noticed that our service men and women come home from deployment and their struggles and hardships go unnoticed. Through this poem, I wanted to let people know that their work is noticed and appreciated. I also wanted to say that through their hardships, they should be commemorated for that as well, not just the uniform.

Clover

Green and bold
Standing alone
Three leaves on your back
As you travel through the grass
Searching for another
Like yourself
Do you wish to be wise like a four?
To be lucky and green
If you dream
You can be
Four and lucky

You are never alone
In this pile of grass
With dirt beneath you
And trees above you
Watch the flowers bloom

Feel the wind
Soak up the sun
Enhance your beauty
You'll have your luck

Don't be sad little clover
One day you'll see
You are unique as can be

Sissy Mae Troy
Philadelphia, PA

Writing is my passion and my favorite outlet. I first began my calling as a writer at Teenink.com, uploading my writing pieces to be shared with the world. My family and my best friends have been my biggest supporters of my writing and continue to encourage me to follow my dream of becoming an author. I am extremely ambitious and will keep succeeding in any way I can.

Winter Solstice of the Soul

In the dark, in the dank,
Closely pressed, rank on rank,
Hear me whimper, hear me cry,
Evil men are passing by.

One is waving pestilence,
One is fracking, deep and dense,
One is sowing windmill farms,
One is calling boys to arms.

Whirling, twirling, jihad, guns,
Grab the priest before he runs.
Tweeting, twerking, hold the place,
Give it up for Facebook space.

Put your baby to the breast,
Hold the dog against your chest,
Make no sound, hit the ground,
Evil men are still around.

Patricia Falter
Sudbury, ON

I am a retired Canadian educator who lives in Northern Ontario with my husband. I have two grown children, a ten-year-old granddaughter, and two grand-dogs, Barney and Zack. Like most of us, I worry increasingly about the state of our world. In the poem, I compare the world of the dark ages, when people huddled in their huts, desperate to avoid attention from the lawlessness without, to the environmental degradation, rise of popular media and chaos of war in our time. Are we returning to an era of complete fear and pestilence? I hope not.

Someday

Times are tough and I have had enough
I am down on my luck but I do not give a crud
I will keep fighting, I will keep trying
I will change things in a hurry
Because life is too short just to worry
Bills are always overdue but I need gas in my car and food
No welfare for me, no thanks, I will pass
I would rather work hard than come in last
Everything is a struggle when working all the time
And being a mom is hard to juggle
I tell myself it will be okay someday
Because education will be my way
No more money being tight, no more putting up a fight
Bills will be paid, food will be made, even money will be saved
My family will have everything they want and need
This is my American dream
My son will be able to have fun
Without being told "No, sorry, we need money, we have none"
This reality is only a few steps away
But for now I must be patient
Try my best, and say, "Someday"

Natasha Monique Shultis
Kerhonkson, NY

Remember and Rebuild

Focus peaks on this page.
Not a word misplaced
Not a syllable misused.
Just the intent, the page, and the hole.
I was born with a wound
At birth, a pain
Which childhood and innocence
Covered from myself,
One which time reminded me of
And revealed, now grown,
Infested, infected, and consuming me whole.
And it ate away, and dissolved the density of my being.

This hole shook me once and now again
This hole broke me once and now again
This hole changed me once and now, again.
It shapes me forever—intimately and infinitely changing me.
And a look down to its place over my heart,
My jerry-rigged and transitory heart,
Taped and glued over the breaks,
Rigid besides the damage.
And this hole and heart
Show me the humanity and frailty
Of this mark, which gives me hope for yesteryears
and days future to come—less sadness. More hope.

Ryan Zenhausern
Fountain Hills, AZ

Humble Mother

The Humble Mother
So tall and so proud she stands
Many days and hours she longs to sit
And take a well-deserved rest
Her shoulders are so weighted down
With burdens of many nations and many worlds
But her burning heart and undying
Love will never allow this lady to take such a rest
Her spirit can never be broken
No matter how many times she's hit, she's
Rained upon, talked about sometimes good
And sometimes bad
She continues to hold her head high
And wear a smile for she is
The mother of billions and the sister of millions
She is the creator of one man's dreams and holds the key to another
Man's destiny
Forever she will remain standing so tall and forever
She will remain so proud
To this dear lady I take my hat off and gesture a bow (Statue of Liberty)

Allison Underwood
Lake Clarke Shores, FL

Ukraine

I am a rich golden field under a sapphire sky
Crying my tears when the soil-heart is dry.
A wild mustang rather dead than be tied;
Losing my head on a frightening ride.
You are my neighbor, my friend I can trust.
While you're hiding your secrets, burying lust.
You are my family, my brother in blood.
A two-headed eagle following scud.
I am a piece of a puzzle you seek to regain
To climb up the ladder to your "rightful" reign.
I'm someone while lost trusted you'd give me aid
And not use my weakness to consume me in raid.
You are a pitiful fool in a costume of king,
A bird wanting flight cutting off its own wing.
Someone who's selling a friendship for land
Once again crushing what took years to mend.
I am my freedom. I am my peace.
Something you're craving to forcefully cease.
You are a bullet that takes away lives.
I am a dolphin making its dives.
You are a gun while I am the sea.
You are so blind... Trust me, I'll make you see!
I am the people who fight for themselves.
You are a child throwing toys from the shelves.
You are a tyrant who only wants more.
I am a country united in war.

Tetiana Nesterchuk
Los Angeles, CA

Let It

The world will
break your heart with
its beauty and
its sorrow.
Let it.
It will be the
best thing you have
ever done.
When the eyes of the heart
are opened, everything
becomes a gift, everything
becomes a blessing.

Mary Campbell
Edmonton, AB

Mary Campbell is an ESL teacher and a poet. She inherited her love of words from her grandmother, who was also a teacher and a poet. She loves the economy of poetry and how it gets to the essence of things. Her poetry is inspired by moments and experiences that touch her heart in some way.

Time Traveler

A dark forbidden world I abide in.
Some deem it to be a blessing as I have been foretold.
I concede it to be a curse in my humanity of eras.
I have seen mortality, famine, destruction of great empires, and eminent wars.
No illumination can be perceived in my humanity.
A shadowy forbidden world I must endure.
I have come to declare it to be a blessing and yet a curse for my existence.
I have seen famine multiplied through the ripples of time.
I have witnessed plagues exterminate the great inhabitants of this world.
I have heard mothers screaming as their children are ripped by mortality.
I have detected elderly laying to rest in their shallow graves.
My eyes are consumed with distress and hopelessness.
My arms have embraced those that have transcended from our humanity.
My hands have revealed to you the wrinkles of times.
My hair is silvery white with the wisdom I have achieved through hands of time.
And yet you want to be collectively of my forbidden dark humanity.
I am only a dream in your psyche, my beloved mortals.
You will fail to remember me soon just as time has forgotten me forevermore.
I am traveler of time.

Ashriel McCloud
Gibsonton, FL

Youth

wrinkles are time lines:
evidence that you have laughed,
frowned,
lived...
physical proof that you have felt the long,
bony claws of Gravity pulling you by the folds in your skin
dragging you down to the ice-ridden soil
until
(on the foggy arrival of November)
he pulls you under
at last.
And when you finally meet Hades,
he offers a sturdy hand to hold
unlike ex lovers and friends,
his embrace is infinite and
with one touch:
peach cheeks,
rosy lips,
and luminescent skin
fade to the same lifeless shade of grey as your legacy
there is no color
that lasts forever.

Raquel Milosavljevic
Burnaby, BC

What Am I

I walk around, but people walk through me.
I stand in a crowd, people look at me but do not see me.
I go see my friends, but they do not see me.
I ask family for one last hug, but they just leave.
Do you know what I am?
I am the ghost of a lonely girl.
I tell you what I am, but you don't listen.
I talk, but I am not heard.

Savannah Victora Mae Spitzer
Woodstock, IL

Ode to the Single Mother

Six little candles upright on a mantle
Awaiting their beloved flame.
Five ready matches wrapped up in their package
Their light has now been tamed.
Four cigarettes in the pocket of her dress
She's never got a moment to rest.
Three potpourris wafting up in the breeze
This isn't a life of ease.
Two lonesome faces with no more spare aces
They belong to the no good places.
One lonely widow sitting there in the window
She strikes the match and waits.

Sarah Ann Coffin
El Dorado, CA

You Are New

We look through poisoned eyes
at a poisoned world and wonder
what went wrong,

when upon the hills of green and
by the glistening streams, the wind
through trees, sang her enchanted song.

In the moments of joy, the sun danced
his jig upon faces in awe,
as they lie in vivid meadows,
laughing in the wonder of it all.

All nature prays release from constant pain,
of being trapped in the confusion
of forgetting her proper place.

Tricked by the illusion of plenty
by what is full of emptiness,
our hearts, on puppet strings, became obsessed.

Remember all, from which rock you were hewn.
Hear this all creation: You have been made new!

Brock T. Fletcher
Jonesboro, AR

Loneliness

As tears of sadness stream down my face
These thoughts of loneliness never seem to erase
I'm fine, content, all on my own
Then something happens and I start to implode
"I can't take it," I say, "I can't take this pain"
Why, oh why, can't it just go away?
But it's always there, like a damn ink stain
I try and I try to run from this place
But then I feel a pull and I slow my pace
Pushing, fighting, doing all I can
This is never ending, am I in quicksand?
"I'm drowning, I'm drowning," I begin to yell
But as I do a silence has fell
I'm voiceless, speechless, I can barely breathe
Where are all the people who are supposed to believe in me?
I can't do this on my own
Please don't tell me that I am alone
"Save me, save me," my last cry for help
But it's too late, I've drowned, without another yelp

Kristen Sloane Robinson
Hendersonville, TN

'Tis the Poetry

'Tis the poetry
For it has seeped into my bones
And filled the cracks within my soul
'Tis the poetry
For I could not stop
Though I had the chance
'Tis the poetry
For my words form works of art
But are still misunderstood
'Tis the poetry
For it is the most beautiful piece of me
The part of me that cannot be hidden
'Tis the poetry
For my sentences are beautifully spoken
Though never good enough for you
'Tis the poetry
For I attempt to describe you
But could never be done
For you are merely a masterpiece
Full of an undiscovered alphabet
Complied of not yet recorded letters
Though I shall not reduce my efforts
For today is only another attempt
To describe you at the utmost perfection
Though I realize it simply cannot be done

Brittany Ann Trevino
Canyon Lake, TX

Floating in Light

Cerulean water,
smooth as glass,
glides gracefully over the velvety skin that remains
anchored down by the aerial weight of a million lucent stars.
Bounded by reality, I gaze into the limitless depth of space,
and where the sea kisses the sky,
the past and future stop to shake hands.
Engulfed by the numbing water,
I listlessly skim my bare skin through its crystalline surface.
Awoken by the swirling water,
multitudes of phosphorescent jellyfish abounding around me
reflect the shimmering pale glow of the burnt-out moonbeams.
As if animated by the breath of the omniscient sea,
the jellyfish synchronically conflate into an ephemeral mass,
before aimlessly drifting away
to further illuminate the somber waves.
For a fleeting moment,
the breadth of the sea is enthralled by the azure incandescence
of an innumerable multitude of vitreous jellyfish.
Without delay, the shimmering gold thread of dawn
infuses its light into the silver blanket of night,
and the burnt-out moonbeams reflecting off the
hyaline limbs of the jellyfish
ardently evaporate into the crystalline air,
imperceptibly waiting for the charcoal twilight to reclaim it.

Maddie Merritt
Centennial, CO

Bliss

Feet dangling over the edge
Grazing over the surface of the water
All noises are distant and coated in a thin layer of peaceful glee
The breeze floating over an edge and flowing through your hair
The air temperature-less
The water underneath your toes is silky
It reflects the sky and the setting sun
The sun that is setting but will never be finished setting
Time is meaningless because it has stopped
Whether you have been there for a lifetime or not at all
That is when you have been there forever
When the world has rotted away
And life ceases to continue
You will remain in place where you know nothing else
The voices meaningless and simple
With so many other souls and so little present
They are occupying meaningless space in another world
Galaxies away
Where one is happy and does not know why
But does not care
Because they are where they want to be
And does it matter how you arrived there?
Bliss

Malini Correa
Niskayuna, NY

Everyday I'm Hustling

Working hard everyday
The first to wake up and the last to go to sleep
Trying to make this money, but my feelings are making me weak
Playing like a savior with no cross or no crown
Allowing other people to run my business in the ground
Sacrificing my life dreams of success
Selling my products for less
Is my love for my family more important than profits?
Give away everything and watch them skyrocket
Soaring and flying high off my mismanagement
Digging a deeper hole for my bereavement
Making bad choices was my everyday thing
Married to it and wore it like a ring
All I have is a business written on paper
Taking everything away like a midnight raper
Menu filled with sweets and treats I tried to tell her
No money and chaos is my best seller
Can I be both a boss and mother?
Separating business and family from the other
Not until I make some changes and improvements
Figure out what's important and *implement*

Nicole Marie Scott
Cahokia, IL

My Dark Passenger

I always feel him there.
I call him my dark passenger,
But I don't think anyone will care.

Sometimes he'll speak to me.
He'll give me advice,
Listen to my words,
But won't let me be free.

I feel his breath down my neck.
He's waiting,
He's calling,
He'll turn my life into a wreck.

I wish he wasn't so deep inside.
There's no way of escaping,
And there's no way of getting him out.
Believe me, I've tried.

Quen Alexander Barkyoumb
Olathe, KS

Inappropriate Affection

Let lust not define us, for we share a kind of mind:
Desire.
A mind linked in between a dark world of carnal knowledge of
Inappropriate affection...
Denial.
To hide behind the truth with rage
Is your definition of reality;
To have your tail in between your legs
Like the coward you sow yourself to be;
To be troubled by reckless thought, but
Only to deny it and proclaim its sexual relation...
Deviance.
You know how to linger a lie,
You love to tease the heart
And spoil the mind...
Devotion.
Malicious wonder corrupts the pervasive mind
To fiend off your prey
To satisfy the thirst for sinister arouse-ment...
I am determined to wake the beast within
To feed my sexual appetite.

Amanda Jasmine Gonzales
Mesquite, NM

Empty

The sky without stars
The forest without trees
The beach without water

A vase without flowers
A frame without pictures
A closet without clothes

A song without sound
The journal without entries
A poem without emotion

Me without you

Amy Hopper
Zachary, LA

After losing a child when he was only eight weeks old, I quickly took to writing poetry to express my emotions and thoughts I had trouble saying aloud. Poetry is my escape. My hope is that readers can benefit emotionally or spiritually from the words I have written. May no one feel they are alone in emotions of life.

Maxwell

Here you come running with flung open
arms to be scooped up totality in our love.
Yesterday mingles together with today.
Who is this we hug with leftover hunger?
Your sweet face is like no other, even your mother's.

Little boy with skin smooth and smile breaking
the sunbeams into rays of life for all to feel.
Run… run quickly while there is time before
we both become too old to play.

Lenore Janet Gordon
San Rafael, CA

Monsoon

I listen to the raindrops, fall from the second floor.
Her cries are getting louder, it's not raining anymore.
Still the raindrops fall, with no end in sight.
I lie in bed and listen, as morning breaks the night.
I try to wear her shoes, only in my mind.
Life can be so fulfillin', yet brutally unkind.
I can't feel her pain, to say I can is cold.
I have never lost a child, hers was four years old.
I lie in bed tonight, sheltered from the storm,
And listen to the raindrops, fall from the second floor.

Ted Mouck
Leaskdale, ON

Painting

A masterpiece painted in a dreary mind
Of a soul that was left behind
A place not to go but there has been kept
In silence now waits in darkness has wept
Hidden without choice
Stolen was their voice
Solemnly their eyes seek
But no strength comes to the weak
A fight fought and lost
Joy and love was the cost
In a mind so scared
Who around would have cared
No one knew no one asked
If not alone they were masked
Decrepit soul of a dreary heart
Awaiting their chance for a brighter art

Mallory Kay Durbin
West Plains, MO

Life Force

You're doing a beautiful job hurting me,
Making me bleed.
My heart it used to sing,
Now it only speaks in eulogies.
You're doing a beautiful job draining me,
Slowly and deliberately,
Intentional or not you're leaving a mark,
But you're doing a beautiful job.
My heart it hurts and my muscles ache,
My mind and eyes long for summer days,
When I only had a care about you,
And all the beautiful things you could do.
Now my blood runs crimson and my tears like quartz,
A beautiful sight when you drain a life force.

Angela Hampton
San Diego, CA

Love Defined

Warm light radiates off thee,
An angel from Heaven above you must be,
Undeniable beauty, even the blind may see,
Shine thine light upon me, and set me free.
Give me your love you hold so deep,
Give me the feeling of thine sacred touch,
And let me feel your love flow and seep,
A lady equal to you: there is nonesuch.
Feel the touch of my love for you,
As my hand is in your hand,
Feel all the beautiful wonders our love could brew.
Feel as I settle this with a golden band.
O my delight in the sight,
When I see you dressed in pure white!

Kyle Everett Wallace
Bartlett, TN

Voices

Voices inside her head
Tell her she's not good enough.
Voices inside her head
Say there's no such thing as love.

Waking up every morning
Has become hard to do.
She is trying to see her life
From a different point of view.

She feels as if she is fading away.
She now lives life from day to day,
Hoping and praying for something to change
Because she is tired of always feeling this way.

She wakes up each morning
Asking if this is the day
That she chooses to fight back
Or allows herself to walk away.

Waking up every morning
Was hard for her to do.
She did her best to see her life
From a different point of view.

Sarah Hope Nelson
Sulphur Springs, TX

I come from a family of six where Christianity is the foundation of our home. Even though this was the case growing up, life got in the way. I grew up being told by peers every day how different and ugly I was. I was made fun of and teased all throughout school, but I am now twenty-three and I have learned a lot about myself. I am a strong, independent woman loved by her friends and family and, most importantly, by the God who gave her life. My name is Sarah Hope Nelson and I have a testimony.

Solemn Wishes

Bliss,
Kindness,
Happiness,
To succumb to this desire is one step toward ecstasy.
Thoughtful,
Generous,
Gratified,
To grasp a memory is nothing short of a blessing.
Meek,
Peaceful,
Repeat,
To want, is to wait, while waiting, anticipate.
Thrilled,
Tickled,
Cheerful,
Relish life as you live it, find joy in the journey.
Pleased,
Content,
Cloud 9,
Be intoxicated in your gratefulness.

A true wish comes as life captivates your eyes.

Timothy Mendel Ivory
Taylorsville, UT

Growing Out

We were like sisters but not like sisters.
We joked we were a covenant.
We skipped class to smoke cigarettes,
exhaling dreams that ended in "O."
At seventeen you held my hand,
while a lucid drunk
tattooed a fairy on my hip, the needle
bringing up beads of blood,
like ancient offerings.
Blood of my blood, born new.
I want to be just like you.
At twenty-two I thought better.
The world called but you just laughed
and hung up. Your reality was your creation
and your creation alone.
At twenty-five you changed your mind.
We were insular fools that could not keep up with you.
Our paths diverged but in the overlap
you found reasons for me to stay.
At twenty-eight I asked to go

further
but you bound me and bound me and bound me.
I removed my tattoo at thirty-two
to erase your existence and be born new.
We were like sisters but we are not sisters.
And may the covenant return to dust.

Yingjun Dougherty
Preston, WA

Grey Sky

December 13

The grey of the sky,
is consuming every piece of me.

It began lingering in my home,
the grey sky is in my home!

The winds of the grey sky have caused,
me to be cold.
I am cold?
The grey skies have made me cold!

No.
For the grey skies have no part of me being cold.
They have not found their way in my home!

I have turned the skies grey,
for I too, am this shade.

I have brought this saddened shade into my home,
I have caused this grey to consume me whole.

The sky is not unhappy,
for I am.

The sky is mere reflection of all my burdens.

Faith Anne Miller
Garden City, MI

Father Time

I asked, "Father Time, are you going to pay a single dime,
for your crime?
I went forward too fast and now you are taking me back.
Your calculations don't add up. My math however, is exact.
Isn't that a fact?
These hips these thighs told lies. I was not yet wise.
All I wanted to do was play. What happened… I dare not say.
Father Time are you going to pay a single dime for your crime!?"
Father Time replied, "I have no money, I have no riches. I
can't give you glory, nor fame.
You will probably die, with many not knowing your name.
But, I can do one thing and one thing only.
The power I do posses is, I can turn back my hands;
this should rectify your misfortune, as well as my crime.
The years since your birth will not show on your face.
It will take another direction.
It will be consumed in another place.
When you speak others will contemplate your age.
Don't become irate or filled with rage.
Simply run, dance and play.
You will get more time to do this then most.
However, it won't last forever.
So, embrace the angelic face only a child could possess.
You need not look grown up; so don't become obsessed.
I will hold my hands back as long as I can,
even when they grow weary.
But the day will come when they give way.
Just be grateful, that day is not today."

Ebony Boone-Faulden
New York, NY

Her Transformation

The woven piece of fabric clutches the figure
sitting in the corner,
dreading the darting stares from the men.
It stretches,
scrambling to cover the curvy body.
Its bright color popping out from
her dark complexion.

Hungry for attention,
it calls her to the dance floor.
The work of one seamstress transforms
the piece into its own soul,
able to brainwash for just one night—
allowing all the worry and pain
to dissolve.
To turn her from a minnow
to a shark
in an ocean of minnows.

Holly Anne Rowland
Becker, MN

How I Came to Love the Storms

every safe haven in my life
has been a decrepit house
sinister simulacrums of home
extending offers of conditional shelter
in exchange for a belief, a freedom, a soul
threatening imminent, spiteful collapse
at first gale, thunder rumble, or rainfall
creaking foundations, leaking roofs, squeaking joints
singing songs of you can never go home again
if you can never leave, pinned underneath

Kassandra Christen Charboneau
Abilene, TX

Fool's Heart Broken

Deep pits of darkness and dwellings of the mole,
Burning flames of hatred casting nets upon the soul.

Brainwashed beings of hopelessness in search of sanity to live by,
Praying God will release the soul and allow the body to die.

For within this flesh lies corruption since was long ago forespoken,
Visions of what's yet to come doth cause this fool's heart broken.

Gary Russell Lemarr
Plano, TX

On wings of my angel, "Afreen," I shall soar to new heights.

My Rock Star

Cover me with kisses.
Hug me through this pain.
Is there really sunshine
after all this rain?

Mama, I love you.
You've always been my friend.
What will I do now?
On whom will I depend?

You have always been my rock,
my confidant, and my strength.
Who will I find now
to go that extra length?

Nobody will ever take your place,
so much love and so full of grace.
And from my heart, you will never be far,
for in heaven, you'll be the brightest star.

Marilyn Montoya
New Kent, VA

I am a retired math teacher. I now care for my mother who has Alzheimer's disease. My mother is an incredible person. She practiced anesthesiology until her retirement at seventy. She has always been an inspiration for me and for women in her field. She was the only woman in her medical school class. She always said, "You can be anything you want to be as long as you're willing to work hard." I cherish every moment with her as we both go through "the long good-bye." My poem was written in tears for my best friend.

Piles

Piles of things I need to do…

Piles of things I need to sort through,
Piles of things I'm collecting for his girls when they are older,
Piles of memories that make me smile and some that make me cry,
Piles of things to toss out of here sooner than never!
Piles with their importance to his lost life,
Surrounded by my piles that mean so much yet not enough.
Memories all carefully placed in piles.

These piles mean your life was important!
You did exist but it's now reduced to piles!
Piles I wish you could crawl out of so I could hold you,
Piles I wish you could come out of and surprise your babies,
Piles which can give no explanation to these questions,
Questions never answered as I rearrange and move these piles
Piles of what you were and what you could have been…

Piles of things I need to do…

Carol Deason
Festus, MO

I'm a mother to three wonderful sons and also a grandmother. My poetry is fueled by grief from the loss of my beloved middle son, Christopher (11/3/1986 –5/11/2014). He died from suicide at the age of twenty-seven after an argument with his wife. He was always under extreme pressure and appears to have had a change of heart about some life choices. So many questions unanswered and such a waste. As a nurse, I deal with life and death everyday. However, nothing can prepare you for the death of a child: the ultimate loss!

Read My Eyes

Read my eyes.
Read my eyes 'cause I'm no good at this lie.
I've got a thousand emotions that I'm trying to defy,
and you can read them all in my eyes.
So read my eyes.
But please, don't lie to my eyes.
For what you say to my eyes,
I hear that inside.
That's when you create the light in my eyes.
And if that light is a lie, it might just break my eyes.
I'm already broken inside.
I'm begging you, don't break my eyes.
Just read my eyes.
Read my eyes.

Brian Caulfield
Rockville Centre, NY

Mrs. Jones

Mrs. Jones was a beautiful woman
Married twenty years
The clock strikes five
Mr. Jones comes home
And has many beers

After the sixth
He raises his fists
Slap… smack… whack
Mrs. Jones's bones begin to crack

Shouting and crying
Neighbors walk by #216
Ignoring the screams
Of Mrs. Jones dying

With an overhang right
Comes the fatal blow to her right cheek
On that frightful night
Mr. Jones put his wife six feet deep

Wanda Hettie Jones
Long Beach, CA

Choices

At one point I wanted it
But now I don't
Because something I wanted so bad
Is what hurt me the most
I have no regrets
Because I got what I wanted
And I took it as a lesson
And decided to learn from it
I'm so very spoiled
So determined to get my way
I guess it's my fault
I asked for it in a way
You left a permanent scar
Just like a tattoo
I hate feeling like this
But I love feeling you
I'm immune to the pain
This is nothing but a game
Although our strategies changed
Things still remain the same
Watch me become a ghost
Right in front of your face
My love is one of a kind
So I'll be hard to replace
And since it's finally over
I'm in a better mental space

Theresa Smith
Philadelphia, PA

I started writing poetry in middle school and as I matured, so did my writing. I published my first book in August of 2013 and it consisted of twenty-five short poems. The book is available on Amazon.com and can be found by searching: Karma Reese Marie. Reese Marie is my writing name because I was teased as a kid about Theresa, and my middle name is Marie. I'm also very proud to say I'm a domestic violence survivor, which makes me living proof that what doesn't kill you, makes you stronger!

Mel-o-dee

I once knew a girl named Mel-o-dee
Yes, Mel-o-dee
And Mel-o-dee hated music,
Just hated it!
If she heard music inside, she'd go outside
If she heard music outside, she'd go inside

But this one day,
Mel-o-dee's town had a party
And there was music coming from all sorts of places
Inside. Outside. Between walls. Even up in her attic!
So Mel-o-dee,
She had an idea,

"I'll just dig a hole in the ground."

And well, she did
Then climbed, buried herself, right in this hole!
And you know something?
Mel-o-dee stopped hearing music, finally!
You know why?
She's dead.

Halimah Harden
Berkeley, CA

The Voice That No One Knows

The voice that no one knows creeps inside my head and torments me
I'm losing it I'm believing you
You're convincing me I'm yours again
Friend or foe It's hard to know a controlling monster a caring friend
Are you warning me to control me, or do you truly love me
The voice that no one knows others try to overhear but it's too low
A humming that only I understand
For such a tiny voice you have a lot of demands
Your survival depends on feeding on inner hope
Taking away what humans need to cope
You see we all at one time acquired dreams
Accomplishing them was only a matter of if we believed
So we dreamed big we dreamed tall never imagining how they
would fall
Until one day the voices told us how dreams are killed by foes
He says even when the host tries to fight the war is all in spite
There are no winners dreams will kill you
A warning I am no longer wanting to heed what if I'm different voice
What if I can accomplish my dreams?
Someone once told me you are an enemy
One I wouldn't expect you are inside of me
So is a heart and a mind and they all betray us from time to time
They call you depression they say you're killing me
My survival is doing the same to you so I ask you kindly set me free
I've heard if you love something set it free do this one favor for me
If you will not go by your own will I'll have to use my force
It's a difficult course but one in willing to take
To set myself free and accomplish my dreams *silence!*

Caitlyn Alyse Lopez
Sacramento, CA

Dark Games

You, yes you, standing alone over there,
Ice tinkling in my half finished drink
As you ponder my beguiling smile and daring stare.
The lights are low, the music seductive, as
I step slowly from the shadow of my lair.

Full moon is out, pulsing my blood inside
Gliding up to you, gaze into dark eyes and ask,
"How would you like a ride?"

There's a special place I know,
Wild, seriously hot, sensual types linger, besides
We can participate in the dancing there
Music of which they play all kinds.

Ah, as I'd hoped you are intrigued.
We are now so hungry to get inside!
My limo drives us smoothly on
We kiss with passionate abandon
Tongues explore, prancing in the black widow's web.

Ah, too bad you, yes you, never arrive.
I step into the dark—alone again.
There, ice tinkling in my half finished drink,
and smile… satisfied…
for now…

Lucinda L. Williams
Sunrise, FL

To the Man I Love

If we had never met,
I wonder what I might have missed if we had never met:
The many special gladnesses my heart cannot forget,
The very precious sunny smile, the love so warm and true,
And all the lovely little things that go to make up you.

I wonder what I might have lost without your helping hand,
Without the many times that you would always understand.
Life wouldn't mean a thing somehow, if you could not be here;
No day could hold a dream worthwhile without your word of cheer.

I wonder what I might have done without your word of praise,
Without your treasured laughter, too, throughout the lonely days.
My troubles all seem little ones; My cares are really few;
And just because I have a friend as sweet and fine as you.

I wonder what I might have missed in hopes and dreams so bright,
And what I might have never known in joyous sweet delight.
I'm sure that through the years ahead I never shall forget,
To thank God in my every prayer because we two have met.

Carolyn S. Allen
Atlanta, GA

A Steel Magnolia

A baby girl is born somewhere in the South
  Her mama is filled with love, pride, determination and compassion
For she knows her baby's journey is just beginning
  And she must be there to guide her along the way.

Soon her baby girl begins to walk and talk
  And her mama teaches her to smile and show love
Reminding her a pretty smile makes everyone feel better
  And she will learn love has no boundaries.

The little girl begins her teens
  Mama says watch your mouth and check your choices
As words can be powerful messengers
  And your choices may be fatal reality.

This young girl starts her new life
  Mama tells her to expect trials and disappointments
For life can get mysteriously complicated at times
  And must be steeled with courage, strength and beauty.

Today, the young girl is a grown woman sitting under her old and enduring magnolia
  Mama's words are blowing through its strong branches and beautiful flowers
Giving her a renewed feeling of pride with a sense of grateful determination
  And a new understanding of what it truly means to be a *steel magnolia!*

Elizabeth Corbin
Marietta, GA

Bear Blood

I stretch and groan,
long overlooked muscles straining in protest
to the unfamiliar movement.
This is my annual retreat
into pain, sweat, and beat of drumming aerobic feet.
My mind dances over the idea that I must have bear blood.
That strong underlying need to forage, gorge, and
feed myself plump to endure the long cold winter
of inactivity.

It must be bear blood,
this recurring seasonal laziness
adding layers of tonnage to my ever-widening body.
Bear blood, passed down through ancestral lines
unbeknownst to my parents.
"Father, tell me the history of your link to the grizzly."
"Your mind works in strange ways, it always has ever since you
were a child. There's no bear blood in me. It must be from your
mother's side."

Why, oh why, does my soul yearn to tighten and tone
only with the lengthening of daylight?
As short skirts and bathing suits reappear into fashion
my blood transforms from bear, into blue.
Blue blood of the vain!

So I stretch and groan,
depriving my body of sweets and fat,
longing for winter and the comfort of my hibernation.

Dawn Riley
Amarillo, TX

New York, New York

New York City
A place to be
Where all can be free
Expressing themselves full of glee
Having a wonderful time
Oh how I wish I could be there
New York City

Charley Jane McKenna
Attleboro, MA

Cure My Loneliness

Take away this anxious feeling
Give me love that has meaning
Take my hand and guide me through
For I'm lost and cannot move
Take away the pain inside
Where memories are left behind
Listen to my sea of words
They come together in a herd
Make my fear just go away
Where there's no more black or gray
Hold me tight in this mess
Please just cure my loneliness

Jennifer Pitts
Lebanon, OK

Granny and the Tara

Cats weren't my favorite thing,
I never thought I could—
Be Grandma to a stray one,
But Katie said I would.

This cunning little kitten,
With eyes as blue as the sky—
Just makes you want to melt,
As sweet as apple pie.

It was meant to be a miracle,
The way we landed her—
First day of our vacation,
The swim really made her purr.

It's Katie's baby sister,
A load off Mary's mind—
It's the reincarnation of Talbot,
The jackpot was won with this find:

My 21st grandchild, Tara.

Yvonne Hoefert
Godfrey, IL

With my six children, five in-laws and nineteen grandchildren, my family is still growing. Living within four miles of each other, some of the "grands" are branching out. Over fifty years ago, my deceased husband and I were fortunate to latch on to a time-share in the Ozarks when Tan-Tara developed. We took our family and their friends eleven times a year and now, since I'm eighty-four years young, I enjoy taking my "golden girl friends," my '66 high school class reunion friends and my family on different occasions. "Tara's Miracle" was discovered there.

Beautiful Soul

As the sun rises
so does your spirit
glimmering and shining as beautiful
as a sunny spring day
oh, how nothing compares—
to seeing a smile on your face
nothing compares to your
beautiful soul.

Kayla Juarbe
East Elmhurst, NY

The Tide

The tide comes rolling in again,
 Crashing on the surf and sand.
And as I watch I wonder why,
 I'm missing you but I cannot cry.
The times we shared have come and gone,
 And we both know I won't be here,
To share those times we once had,
 To watch the waves crash in the sand.

Gary Baab
Hudson, OH

I wrote this when I was eighteen and a Marine in San Diego, California, far away from a small Ohio town. I married a California girl and returned back home. We are blessed with six children and eight grandchildren.

The Runner

As I lived this life of sin and shame,
I ran to fulfill this yearning.
From drugs to alcohol and gambling games,
Unsatisfied my soul still burning.
I tried to pray from time to time,
But Satan kept winning the fight;
I now had a habit, life filled with crime
I ran both day and night.

Now with two yearnings, my soul still burning.
Life was too far out of reach,
I had given up on hope, and into dope.
But I remembered a message my brother preached,
Christ loves you, Christ cares and He's always there.
He shed His blood, for your sins.
Stop running for Satan, 'cause he don't care.
Try Christ and believe, and you'll win.

I ran even more till I opened the door,
To a cell in a little county jail.
I had committed a crime, and could get lots of time
And no one to go my bail.
Old Satan is still fighting, while I'm facing the charges,
And he seems to think he will win
But now I have Christ, who's come into my life.
So I'll keep running from sin.

Minister Walter Green
Petersburg, VA

Divisions

The pot melts no longer, the path has been subtle.
The divisions are clear; there is no rebuttal.
The dream of a great man, let our people unite,
Is but cliché for deaf ears, whether heard left or right.

Ignorance knows no color, with great brush it has spread.
The miles have been travelled, the words have been said.
For a time solvency, it seemed to be in check.
Though lasting not too long, the train destined to wreck.

A man in high office, proof that most did not care.
Divides with stout speaking, and so many unaware.
What hope is there in change, when it creates such hate?
Fundamental in nature; no return, it's too late.

But not just about skin, it's what some have—some not.
Poor decisions the cause? No, just fairness it's thought.
Won't do something to change; no American dreams.
Hard work and honesty, simple concept it seems.

Someone has to provide: entitlement nature.
For years laws are passed. Thank the legislature.
Those still in the ghetto, many still in the trailer.
No matter what's given, it won't solve the failure.

A few prop the many. The future is quite clear.
A collective group bound, freedom never seen near.
History repeats well, make the same decisions.
Separate not equal, walls forming divisions.

Jason Bricker
Mitchell, NE

To the Vagrant

The sun blazes the terra-cotta, blanched
leaves print themselves on the bungalows.
Nights past she paints with the lacquer of hindsight,
my negotiated tongue wilting in our wake.
The pangs of lost mornings, swords in hand
to shred their soil. She turns, to feel
Alone or, hand in hand, and scales the waves
burying our daggers in their rhythm.
The tide—based on moon's breath—
proceeds, recedes, gulping down her infernal ghosts.
Upon the shore, a cutting luminance dances across
sand, clenching to the souls it sees ripe;
There I am, the same sand chafes my palms
as I contort my heart into pieces to fit
Into heaven, or hell, who cares?
I've seen before sycophants like her
Who ache for wings of vagrancy; yet,
who upon flight, buckle in the wind
Careening back down, vulture
eyes searching for a vacant chariot
To drive her home, to the sun, a
shadow through twisted trees.
In vain! Even the birds know to fall
back to the ground to collect their
Organic fortunes, patter against my sill
And laugh at the eagerness of lost grace.

Derek Kelly
Alpine, NJ

"To the Vagrant" was inspired by my first girlfriend, Sarah, who left home at a very young age to travel the country and chase the ever-illusive dream of finding herself. The poem was conceived by the image of a bird "buckling" upon first flight. This image led the construction of the poem: I used it as a metaphor for Sarah and her first failed attempt at flight/leaving home.

Transit of Venus

She appeared like a wild rose: blooming in a distant corner of some silent, neglected, and aged garden.

The sudden, improbable appearance of bright color being made more brilliant against the dulled tapestry of dried foliage.

Then, this unexpected blaze of color dimmed and was gone.

Should I now mourn this transit of impermanent joy, or revel in the memory and hold it dear, tucking it away in that special place that makes us human?

Should it not join other secret tapers glowing in that gloom of memory when darkness seemed forever, lighted from those brief feelings of warmth felt, and gladly accepted, as temporary shelter from a cold world?

Likewise, wasn't the muted garden crowned and exalted by that single, transiting bloom… even if only for a brief moment?

H. Howard Swink
Norfolk, VA

Mom

As encouraging as the wind
  beneath a bird's wing;
As comforting as the sound
  of angels, when they sing;
As accepting as our ears
  when church bells ring;
These are the things, most in
  my life, you bring.

Your words of wisdom, always
  so very clear;
With a helping hand, you are
  always near;
Because of you, I face challenge,
  with little fear.

Your strength, good character and
  loving ways;
I strive to have, throughout my days.

Lisa Moffett
Gulfport, MS

On His Passing

You hug his sweater a little tighter
And wonder why, it always rains
When your world's under the weather.
Pulling clichés from clouds, like how
Since the other green one shattered,

Now there's only one chair
By the green plastic table, so
No second chance can be had.
You fiddle with his ring
And press your face against the glass,

Watching. Water trickles through the cracks
Through wooden boards on the deck, and
Your hair is in knots, splitting ends,
In the silence, in your head.
You press your hands against the glass

And catch yourself. The thought,
Asking where the time has gone,
If rain could somehow fall up
But when tears pour out from the sky,
They press back into the earth

And eventually forget.

Karis A. Bedey
Bozeman, MT

Motel

Living in one room.
Motel.
Being so isolated
But, yet in the hustle, bustle world.
Motel.
Knowing no neighbors
Yet people all around.
The quiet, the silence.
Motel.
All the people coming…
All the people going.

Much like the world in general.
Being at the doorstep
Yet so far, far away.
Being so close
Yet so far, far away.

That's the way it's always been
That's the it will always be
Being at the doorstep.
Yet so far, far away.

Living in one room.
Motel.
Being so isolated.
But yet in the hustle, bustle world.
Motel.

James Brinkman
Bismarck, ND

Beans Are Gems

They lay down nitrogen
And raise up protein
Pretty while alive
But overlooked dried

Beans nourish
Even after they flourish
A can of beans stored up
Is insurance against emptiness

Such a wonderful storehouse
Of necessities is a bean
True, cheap though
Beans be

Their passing through
Can often result in a smelly
Poof, making the bean eater
Seem like a goof

But the truth is that beans
Are gems whose twinkling
Annoys only the poor
In diet

Kevin Blakemore
Aurora, IL

An Illuminated Birth

The night of the Nativity
Shines in angel-driven text.
It brings us signs—as seen in dreams.
This story lights a timeless quest.

With awe plain shepherds know while still
Angels voice God's *peace* decree.
They seek, where told, a savior birth.
The crib scene beams "simplicity."

Now, we as shepherds mind our world.
Night—*right now*—holds heaven's herald.
As we each heed our angel call,
One finds at core a savior child.

E. Engates White
San Jose, CA

Mother Above

Mother above, I send my love
To you with all that's sweet.
And dear and kind, with you in mind,
I'll smile, I'll tear, I'll weep.
I'll miss your face I held that day
In my hands, you looked at me
And I at you, for a moment or two
To hold that moment close.
And the hug we shared
Would be the last we'd have.
And the one I'll remember most.
The Lord gave me a beautiful mom.
The Lord has taken her soul.
Blessed be the name of the Lord
As mom blessed us all.
I love you Mom, Tommy.

Tom Seib
Omaha, NE

Awesome Is Today!

The morning light cometh in on a dew
shining grass that made the light and
sparking a new.
Oh what breeze that cool and
perfect too.
Oh how new it all seems.
The red birds, begin to sing, what
sounds like a beautiful spring.

Awesome is today!
The morning is today that will go
away!
A new beginning through the day.

Our honeysuckle smells so sweet,
the flowers are all so upbeat.
Of course the bees begin to play.

Awesome is today!
Our world will return another all
the more we have to share and
say.
Glory, beautiful, wonderful
awesome is today!

Francis Solomon
Corsicana, TX

I was born in Lubbock, Texas, on March 28, 1956. I have a great personality. I do have faults. My very traces are courage, passionate, so spontaneous, and personal. I get fired up when it comes to a challenge, and always will to achieve my goals. Depending on no one else except myself, I'm working hard. It helps you: strength, intelligence, just courage, I am, I will, I shall. Getting the pleasure from reading, writing, and word finds. It's like a puzzle, another form of art. I am there in the moment. Sometimes waves of lines come to me, then I write them down. I enjoy my poems. I'm glad to share with my family, friends, and church family, giving them the gift of love. I do indeed love the gift that's in my heart: sweet, sweet life. Unforcing, the beauty of it all. That really can come to life.

Daybreak… Awaiting Tomorrow

Do you ever awaken
As your heart is revealing
You must hide all day long
Broken dreams you're concealing?
Rubbing eyes… looking brave…
Every tear you're erasing.
And you're praying for courage,
Knowing heartaches you're facing.

As the day then unfolds
With its hours so endless,
Are you struggling through,
In your heart feeling friendless?
Think about this, dear friend,
In your journey each day,
New paths can appear!
God indeed knows the way.

Tomorrow, the daybreak
Once dawned, can reveal
Many answers unfolding,
Old wounds then to heal.
Reach out now to God.
Really know He loves you.
On His strength, do depend.
With His help, you'll get through.

Nancy M. Walker
Manteo, NC

Loss of Talk

Talk to me, doctor,
Tell me what's wrong—
No paper in the copier?
So, no information to take along!

We must get back to basics—
It's called conversation.
Since when have vocal cords
Become just space occupation?

Helen Pokrifcak
East Chicago, IN

Pessimism

To many disappointments gathered
Lots of ragweed too little heather
Makes one ponder if it's narrow
To be like the tiny little sparrow
With no thought of the day or tomorrow
Not a trace of worry we know or sorrow
If today is full of roses and sunshine
Will the morrow bring hurt and showers?
Never a sweet thought of realism
Without the assurance of pessimism

Mary Swiggett
Lebanon, TN

Deadly Desires!

Yes, I'm married to a loving wife
And, we also have some kids,
I was secretly meeting with Mrs. Jones in my church
And, I thought that our secret was really hid!
I've preached to others about being faithful to their spouse
But I was in for a rude awakening
When my secret life was turned inside out!
Many times I slept with Mrs. Jones
For, I thought I had her husband's trust,
I was tempted by my own desires
So I gave in to my desires of lust
Mrs. Jones and I had many secret meetings
Even, as I preached to others God's word
Yet, myself, I didn't heed
Smiling faces do tell lies
And, it hurts, being deceived
Stolen water is sweet
Then, one day Mr. Jones learned about my sleeping with his wife
Mad as hell with a loaded shotgun he came to church
But, I didn't know it would cost me my life
"Deadly Desires!"
Don't get entangled
Drink water from your own well
For stolen waters will take your life
And, send your soul to hell!

Margaret A. Richard
Lake Charles, LA

Never Give Up

Whatever circumstances you're going through or pain that you're in,
Don't throw in the towel, never let the devil win.
God is bigger than any situation you may have to face,
He will win all your battles in this life's race.
You may be knocked down but not knocked out,
So give praise to the Lord as you sing, dance and shout.
Pull yourself out of that depression and trust in the Lord,
He'll fill your life with gladness so you won't be bored.
Stop complaining all the time, make your life sweet,
Tell yourself you are a winner, never accept defeat.
Just remember to be depressed is a choice,
So be happy and joyful as you lift your voice.
Lift it to the heavens and lift it here on earth,
Fill your life with laughter, joy and mirth.
For in this life you never know what lies ahead,
One day you're here, the next you may be dead.
Never let the devil steal your joy or health,
For he hates to see you prosper or acquire any wealth.
God will always make a way even when there seems to be none,
So stop the worrying and trust in Him, He'll fill your life with fun.
Just remember all good things come to those who wait,
So wait upon the Lord, show Him you have courage, strength and
faith.

Gloria Dean
Spring Hill, FL

I was born in the Caribbean island of Trinidad and grew up with a love for writing. At the age of thirty-three, I was told by medical doctors that I was dying. My soul was trapped in the deep darkness of fear, hopelessness and depression. In the midst of this despair, the Lord Jesus Christ started inspiring me to write poems. Prior to this, I'd never written a poem before in my life. He is my inspiration for my poems and I give Him all the glory. I am eternally grateful to Jesus for saving me.

Sands

Instead

What is this in me? It's digging up darkness.
Instead of one hundred I only feel like a fifty
Because this harness has me bound with no progress.
Are you still with me? I feel like something is missing
So I'm waiting and debating whether I should allow shifting.
Yes, I do need fixing. There's no denying that.
Fact of the matter is I'm wrestling right now.
Instead of resting right now, my mind is going wild
Like a gorilla in a cage. Instead of dropping my sights down,
I aim and I bang to try to take what I want to claim.
It's all vanity and chasing selfish desires is leading to insanity,
Which is damaging your holy empire. I'm a savage scavenging
Your gifts without walking through the fire. I want blessings with no struggle,
And no testing. And the best thing I'll do for you is speak
For a minute or two. Instead of giving dues to the fuel that
Keeps me, I have idols left and right, so I'm not seeking
Straight. What's my case? A bad case of the "idol-itis"
Because I'd rather give to something that doesn't give back.
I won't give my all over to the one that fully benefits me
Like a revolver with no kick-back. You are the very genesis of my
Existing, so, instead of resisting, I should allow the grace
That abounds in abundance control me simply. It's funny how empty
I can be without it. Without a doubt, I no longer want
This in me, so instead, I permit you to gouge it.

Anthony Lockhart
Fort Pierce, FL

Breathing: A Nonfiction Poem

When the house was dark and very quiet
Way in the middle of the night

My heart starts pounding loudly in my chest
I knew then there would be no rest

After a while I hear the breathing, coming toward my bed
Slowly, I will reach down and pull the cover over my head

Lord, don't let the breathing come tonight, silently I pray
But the breathing always came, before the crack of day

When it was over I would lie there and cry
A voice inside of me saying, O Lord just let me die

I knew the breathing would never stop as long as I was there
I was just a little girl, wondering how much more could I bear

In my mind I began to think, please dear Lord let it be day
So the breathing will soon go away

But the breathing would come when everything was quiet
O, Lord, I silently pray, please spare me the breathing tonight

Elizabeth Taylor
Macon, GA

The Thoughts I Have of You

The thoughts I have of you
Are precious in my mind,
The thoughts are there to stay
The thoughts of you are kind.

The thoughts I have of you
Are memories as well as dreams,
The memories are forever priceless
While the future is to be foreseen.

The thoughts I cherish
About the present and the past,
Go hand in hand with love
Because forever I know it will last.

As I go through life
The thoughts of you are best,
They make me smile at night
When I lay my head to rest.

The thoughts of you are deep
With every breath I breathe,
I think you're the best of everything
You are certainly what I need.

Brian Lawson
Nauvoo, AL

Acrostic Poem

Delicate
Elegant
Exquisite
Rambunctious

Lizzy Hagler
Gilmer, TX

Liquid Love

To my greatest love,
Joy consumes my soul when I see you.
Your aroma floats through my senses.
Your touch is warm and comforting.
My body craves your goodness!
I would have no motivation if I had not found you.
Other people yearn to have you, because of how you open their eyes.
You can be both light and sweet then strong and dark.
You make me stay up all night!
Often my lack of sleep leaves me regretting my lust for you,
But when I see you in the morning, I feel alive again.
My dearest coffee,
I love you.

Katrina Bates
Mission, BC

Untitled

On a blustery, wintery March day in the northern province city of South Bend in the state of Indiana, North America, on the third day of the third month in the year of 1930 A.D.
A gentle and meek creature was born into the world
This quiet and peace loving mouse lived her long life caring and sacrificing
For others, human or creature, with compassion without complaint
As often happens in a harsh and hard world
The predators and parasites seek out and torment
Any creature who chooses gentleness and peace avoiding conflict and controversy
These bullies endlessly seek out and torment
The gentle of spirit, the caregivers of kindness
Eighty-two years pass
A sound is born, barely heard
It is quiet, gentle, and meek at first
The sound grows and grows
All the gentle creatures stop to listen
They are awed and curious
The birds stop singing
Rabbits and squirrels raise their ears
Dogs and cats stop playing
Children stop fussing all listen
The noise grows and grows what is it?
Now it is clear and they know the gentle and meek mouse named Delores is
Roaring like a *lion*
Her heart is quiet, peaceful, and brave and the bullies are silent at last

Mike Dunivan
Kokomo, IN

I was born in 1949 and given a year to live; I did not die. My writing influences are Hemingway, Stanley Kunitz, and Jim Harrison. When I learned of my mother's long suffering from family bullies I was both heartbroken and full of rage; tears and words flowed as I typed. I did not add or delete a single word. My mother's health is fragile; she does not fear dying as she lives quietly with her beloved cats and dog, trying to harvest happiness before her short visit (and ours) on earth ends. The bullies are silent at last.

Death's Pace

Quick, sudden, in a lighting flash, the blink of an eye
Unexpected, startling, shocking, here—then gone.
Departed
Slow, methodical, a snail crossing the street, an icicle
Melting, a flower bud unfurling in the night,
Departed slowly
A slow motion movie, long drawn out suffering,
Unmerciful pain, agonizing hours, a leaky
Drippy faucet, endless nights, unfulfilled goals,
Anxiety, worry, so much left unfinished.
Praying, hoping, grieving, bedside vigils.
Mourning the not-yet departed.
Death waits...
Dear merciful heavenly Father
Hear me in the depths of my soul.
Let me be worthy to enter your kingdom
Release me and take me home.
I pray my loved ones find comfort
In my awaited journey to
Heavenly eternal peace.
As with the rising sun,
Let us be peaceful.
God be with you.

Jean Biagi
Sacramento, CA

In Response to "A Frail Angel's Cry"

I'm sorry Guardian Angel
for all the hurt I've caused
your wings are ripped and torn,
from all the wrong I've done

Today is the beginning of a reality for me
I surely see the things you said,
while I was in my sleep
never did I stop to look above myself, and
little did I hear when you tried to speak
I now realize why you brought my life
to my attention in a dream

The bruises that you shielded,
have now brought me shame
leaving you torn and worn
have caused me so much pain

The instant that I heard "A Frail Angel's Cry"
Tears filled my eyes, as I began to see my life

I gave my word to you that I would
truly change
I'll show you love and beauty,
and you'll be proud at last

The life that I've been living has
never been at ease
Since you had that talk with me
I now feel at peace

Mary Jefferson
Hanford, CA

I was born in Houston, Texas, raised in California (Monterey County), where all my children were born. I'm a mother, grandmother and a widow. I often write poems for family and friends, but had never entered a national contest. When I read "A Frail Angel's Cry" it inspired me to answer back to my angel watching over me in the life I've lived. I'm excited and grateful that my poem was chosen to be in the book Beyond the Sea.

I Shall Not Fall

When the road is rocky
And you get hurt
I shall be your crutch.
When times seem their darkest
And you cannot find your way
I shall be your light.
When the sky turns black
And the wind blows hard
I shall be your shelter.
When the day seems to burn
With the heat of a thousand suns
I shall be your shade.
When you get lost in the world
I shall be your guide.
When all is said and done
You shall stand with me at your side
And with one mighty breath say
I shall not fall.

Kathy Lemke
Dwight, IL

Where I'm From

I am from the valleys of Manteca to the small town of Morgan Hill. I am from the juice of the grapes and the sweetness of the jelly. I am from the grease the tractor spouts plowing fields of my Opa's walnut orchard. I am from the walnut ranch that is slowly dying of age. I am from the tree-lined streets of Willow Glen, and the neighborhood of Cambrian. I am from the best weather in the country—the bay area, home sweet home. I am from crafty chess and chewy, warm chocolate chip cookies from Dad and Mom. I am from creators and builders I call aunts and uncles. I am from badminton and knock-out, basketball and running. From Friday night with friends allowing me to play and be myself over and over again. From slumber parties with Nerf wars and late movies... ingredients of a great birthday. Everyone knows I love a birthday party with presents and cake. I am from Non and Papa, my other home with fabulous pastas in brilliant colors. I am from Papa's wondrous garden that he took care of until cancer took him from us. I am from Opa and Granny's ranch where many come to visit, tractor rides and more. I am from a band of three—Nicholas, Olivia and me. I am my brother's loyal friend and complex foe, but I am simply Olivia's big bro. I am the leader, the boss, the big cheese, when my five-year-old sister says I can be. I am from pillow fights and bedtime stories but I really enjoy late night treats. I am from a family who enjoys a warm fire, and yes, I build them well. I am from a family that likes to travel—Italy is swell. Fishing with Dad and trip to Alcatraz were adventures with Auntie JuJu and Non. The dueling pirates of Disneyland are the bomb. I am from a family who likes excitement... from learning and doing. I am from these moments.

Ryan Scadden
San Jose, CA

My poem started out as an English assignment. My grandfather passed away a couple months before I wrote it. I took the opportunity to think about where I came from and the people in my life. I don't consider myself to be a great writer but for some reason writing it seemed easy for me. I'm sure there are many others who have great stories, however, most aren't fortunate enough to enter this contest and be published. I'm thankful for this opportunity and hope you enjoy this poem as much as I've enjoyed writing it.

In Retrospect

Ah… my friend
we really had it on…
playing out the game
dancing out the song.

We sang… We played…
all the while believing
no inning to the game…
an encore to the song.

The game was time…
The song was youth
and ah… my friend
we shared in their abuse.

Would it be different
could we have known…
the game… we'd lose…
the song… become
a bitter bitter tune.

My friend?

Patty McKay
Vicksburg, MS

The Blue Sapphire Heart

Cradled within the palm of my hand
rests the heart of my daughter.
Like gentle waves upon the sand,
like a master potter,
I smooth, I shape,
I cut, I carve,
I polish, I perfect,
until her heart gleams with glory,
and she is spotless, without defect.

Her heart was once a lifeless stone,
tragically broken, abandoned, alone.
Rough and hoary,
left with no hope for her story.

Then I spotted her with utmost delight
and saw the majesty I destined to be—
a radiant gem robed in the hues of my sea.

She is my blue sapphire heart—
blue as the heavens which display my son,
blue like the mighty oceans deep.
Forever she shall rest in my faithful keep.

All day she brilliantly shines,
to praise me for my love divine.
For there is nothing else she desires
my love protects her through every fire.

What once was broken is now made new.
Will you let me create beauty within you?

Analiese Majetich
Orlando, FL

Untitled

We're going to go far away
Up into the trees where there are five little bees
The sun shines while the clouds are out
Let's be thankful and not have a doubt
Where the flowers blossom and rose bushes sway
Please don't take that away
Let's all be thankful let's all be grateful
That life is in the palm of our hands
Let's now wash them with the dirty sand
To enjoy the fruits of our future
With each and every day and moment a little pronounce
This is life I announce

Crystal LaSorsa
Poughkeepsie, NY

Burr

I have never been one to flirt with troublesome boys
yet in the season of snowflake water
there is no warmth but his skin, like fur,
and the Lord says, "Burr."

Latreece Fulton
Chelan, WA

Latreece Fulton is an eighteen-year-old from Chelan, Washington. She dreams of being a poet and fiction writer and finds everything in life writable.

The Game

Two can play at that game
In which there are no winners
Only losers and silence
Deafening worse than the roar;
Separating like same
Magnet poles tearing
Everything apart between;
Rules upside down and
Fairness residing only
In children and frightened pets;
When a simple sorry
And understanding
From both might restore, but
Incapable due to
Perceived threats and hurts
Never intended or
Which even occurred.
Breaking into waves on
That beach where vows exchanged
Twelve years ago this day
Into meanings countless
Against sand receding,
Forgotten forevermore.

Daniel McGee
Sacramento, CA

A poet at heart, Daniel D. McGee is an attorney practicing in Sacramento, CA, where he resides with his loving wife and their three children. Among other things, he is currently working on a collection of poems including several examining the moral, spiritual and creative conflicts inherent in the practice of law. He draws much inspiration from his practice, as well as his family, friends, Midwest upbringing, and the beauty that is the Sacramento Valley and surrounding Northern California region.

The Winds of Time

the winds of time so softly blow
and golden leaves begin to fall
the evening shadows slowly lengthen
it seems I hear the master's call

the days are getting shorter
and the breeze is getting cold
remember me my darling
when you recall the days of old

I'll be waiting by that river
where the crystal waters flow
there we'll see no shadows
and the winds of time won't blow

Carl Melgaard
Dunseith, ND

Sleuth

Seek in a small creek a wood and mud dam where water
like champagne from thousands of magnums cascades—falling
water
more original than the Wright one.

Pry open an oyster clinging tightly with all its might.
When tug of war is done, it slurped down; notice inside
the half shell its bruised thumbnail.

On a cool fall morning, locate a spider web
cast over blades of grass, a collapsing miniature big-top,
the circus fleeing invisibly.

Awake, roam through a still, dark house,
walk in on a full moon invading an unlit room,
examine the window knocked to bare floor.

Make note of August, its unspoiled golds peacefully feeding on
hot light
ignorant of calamity. Observe them in October, heads bowed,
bodies slumped, shriveled, mummified

and remember they will rise. Explore a cove
of an upended tree, carpeting the entrance last year's leaves.
Crawl in, question the roots: they speak candidly.

If you must—a last resort—go to the vole.
Depend on a small spade; gently turn him up.

Linda Kennedy
Mechanicsville, VA

A Thoughtful Person

You are a thoughtful person,
Who is busy every day
With people who depend on you
And many roles to play.
But even so, you find the time
For friends and family,
Giving them the best you can
With warmth and honesty.
That's why it brings more loving pride,
Than these few words can tell,
To see you do so much in life,
And do it all so well.
"So I give to you a tribute:"
A handful of roses, tied in a bow,
A pocketful of memories, whereever you go,
And
A sky that's full of sunshine,
To lighten up your way.

Jean Herek
Greenfield, WI

Pastel Shades of Us

Admiring the sky as the sun set,
The clouds blushed,
Bashful of their beauty.
I turned to the vacant space beside me
In hopes to meet your gentle eyes,
Wishing you could appreciate
The aftermath of a day
Almost as radiant as your smile.

The sea breeze kisses my skin
But I wish it were your lips grazing mine
Instead of the air whispering into my ears.

An infinity of sand grains hug my feet,
But do not compare to the warmth
In my heart,
When your arms encompass me.

The sun edges the horizon,
Falling down falling down falling
And then all at once,
The same way I fell for you.

Emily Anne Frigon
Plaistow, NH

Weak

Strong in love
But weak alone
Blinded by fiction
Hit with love's stone

Bridges break
Then come the waterfalls
How could love so weak
Break down walls this strong

Oh… you love me?
I could hardly tell
You left me weak
Because only the strong prevail

Zamyria Teyanna Harvey
Grovetown, GA

Never Ending Peace

I went with the hounds, trailed their padded paw prints
while we looked for the fallen.
There wasn't much left in the massacred-field rose color,
only parts of memories that remained with those who were numb.

One side maintaining a dream of ordered anarchy and the other
for a bloodied freedom.
Dog tags knew their time was limited when this makeshift rebellion
came knocking at their shared door.

Sides were no longer sides when these bodies were buried beneath
one another.
The mutts' ears perked with anticipation, as did the smoke filled
breaths that poured out from their muzzle.

Our job is not that of coroner, but that of a diplomat for the dead.
They were faces that I once knew, with lights inside their eyes,
now they are all just dead hearts.
The dogs stopped neck deep in stacks.

Hayden Simpson
Kalamazoo, MI

She

Passion is not poison or evil,
Nor is she a sensual lyric
Or a Picasso on an easel
She is twisting and branding
And cannot be simply described
She is contradicting and confusing,
And at times, full of lies
Her captivating charm is what sets our conscious beside,
Your mind says, "No more,"
But she pleads, "Keep on trying"
What is seen and what is felt
Can no longer be tied
Because passion argues,
The more you feel, the more you find
Because passion argues
That passion is beautiful, and is kind
Because passion argues
That passion is healthy,
But won't confess to her toxic times
Passion's purpose is unknown,
Yet she controls all of our lives
Through the smiles,
Through the cries,
Until the day we are called to say our good-byes.

Cheyenne Elyse Evans
San Antonio, TX

October 17, 2014 (1:12 AM)

While others were living,
I had to force myself
to live

While others were smiling,
I had to force myself
to smile

And it hurt

That the daily things,
were taken away from me
by some crooked chemical imbalance,
we call depression

How did I survive
that mess of a life?

Ashmi Singh
San Francisco, CA

Marry Me?

Roses are red
Violets are blue
I love your hugs
You love me too

Roses are red
Violets are blue
Give me a kiss
And a ring too!

You wear black
I'll wear white
You'll be my man
And I'll be your wife

Taylor Melissa Long
Glendale, AZ

Cutting

Razor crying out for blood
Comfort, like the comfort of a baby blanket
Tears roll down her emaciated cheeks
Turning to her razor
She has no friends left

Murphy Lynne Jonas
Wichita, KS

She

She… she was my world…
Her energy giving life to life itself
Impossible to tame though many have tried
Her skies, limitless, her oceans run deep
I dive, head over heels into the abyss
In search for treasure worth more than gold
To find her world that was too heavy to hold
And I sank with it…
My world no longer the center of her universe
But merely a speck on the Mona Lisa
I loved it when she smiled…
A smile that doesn't belong to me
But to the world

Ezra Ezirim
Winnipeg, MB

I Dreamed About Mother

Last night I dreamed about Mother
Oh! What a perfect delight.
She took me all over heaven,
It was a wonderful sight.
She told me all about Jesus,
And that he's coming again.
She told me how he came to earth
To save every man.
We walked down the streets of gold,
The half has never been told,
And if we meet her there some day,
We never shall grow old.
We will set down at Jesus' feet
And worship, his holy name.
No one will try to seek
Their fortune or their fame.
For everything will be complete
No need of wealth up there.
For Jesus is the king of kings,
He will meet our every care.

Virginia Bensen
Albertville, AL

Speak to Me

Speak to me ye mountains and trees,
Speak to me of a reign that shall be.
Speak to me ye whispering winds,
Speak to me, speak to me of Him.
Speak to me, speak to me.
Speak to me ye rushing streams,
Speak to me of the redeemed,
Speak to me ye river beds,
Speak to me of who stood my stead.
Speak to me, speak to me.
Speak to me ye glorious land,
Speak to me of my master's hand.
Speak to me ye eagles that soar,
Speak to me of shekinah outpour.
Speak to me, speak to me.
Speak to me ye sun, moon, and stars,
Speak to me of who we are.

Kathleen Todd
Coventry, CT

Breast Cancer Awareness Month

Breast Cancer Awareness Month is in October, which also
celebrates Halloween fall foliage.
Raising funds and awareness should occur year-round and not just
in October. Eliminate all kinds of cancers and pains in the world.
Actively participate in fund-raising events like festivals and dinner
dances. Start your own mission by collecting donations from local
community members.
Take charge of this cause with the pink ribbon seal as well as
pink clothing. Cancer is a very stressful and excruciating thing to
experience. Attack it before it attacks you by getting screened and
treated. Never forget that fruits and vegetables are anti-cancer.
Capture every opportunity to eat healthy foods.
Enter a nutritious lifestyle of proper eating, sleeping, and exercise
habits. Run or walk in a 5K marathon fund-raiser for this worthy
cause. Awareness leads to benevolent acts of donating hair to
Locks of Love. Women who cannot donate hair to make wigs will
contribute money. Acts of kindness and gratitude come in various
forms and styles. Realize that there is more than just one way of
helping others. Even those who are uncomfortable with shaving
their heads can just donate braids.
No contribution is ever too small as every little bit counts when
accumulating funds.
Everybody should unite when making a friendship quilt of hope,
faith, and peace.
Sisters and brothers can all join in making a positive difference.
Sing Martina McBride's song "I'm Going to Love You Through It"
to show moral support.

Hilary Fergenson
Tenafly, NJ

Hilary has been very passionate about art and writing all her life and immensely enjoys conducting monthly poetry meetings at the Tenafly Public Library. Hilary was inspired to write a poem about breast cancer awareness to honor some of her beloved friends who are survivors. Aside from writing poetry, Hilary does recreation therapy with disabled adults and teaches autistic children and teenagers. She also values spending quality time with family and friends. Hilary has a bachelor's degree in studio arts from Goucher College in Towson, Maryland, and a master's degree in elementary education from Fairleigh Dickinson University in Teaneck, New Jersey.

Two of My Ex-Boyfriends Are Dead

Two of my ex-boyfriends are dead,
And I'm not 40 yet.
They were both just 23.
Sometimes they visit me.
They say, "Time ticks different here."
Faster, like a circle, less linear.
One died in a car, one died in a war,
I'm not the same person I was before.
When all is calm, I feel them there.
You can probably see them in my distant stare.
Both live within me like roots of a tree.
The earth is my youth, and they ground me.
They were only 23.
Somehow I got past, the *why*, not the *when*,
Don't think I'll ever be the same again.
Flames seem brighter, life, more vital,
Smaller things smaller, there might be no tomorrow.
After all their visits, the message is clear.
They say it's much, much, much harder here.
Under the same full moon, there's so much beauty.
But we're too busy doing our duty.
Working hard to be rich, fighting for a cause.
In our little, linear world, we forget how to love.
Given time is not linear, then what is age?
But a numerical concept keeping us caged.
Time is relative, we're too human to see,
The wisdom in this can set us free.

Kaitee Page
Dallas, TX

Kaitee Page is a musical artist and author, from New York, currently living in Dallas, TX. Please visit KaiteePage.com.

Blue

Summer's sweltering sweet kiss bites into sun drenched
flesh... under its inviting rays pleasure is its immense
heat. White heat much to bare leaves the body wanting...
tempting blue coolness to refresh, revive the senses.
In a quite pool honey tanned limbs tip tap at the water's edge,
ending fevered tempt to rise no more.
Blue in the sound of your laughter as you dance in a misty
rainbow, sprang from a lazy garden hose. Blue heavenly sky
looks back at the face of one of its own as she lay in comfort
on a lush slope, the picture in itself as beautiful as any
Monet hanging in the Louvre.
Blue is the shimmer of soulful eyes how they imagine a world
worth believing in. The colors of life is a cascade of the many
when I see her I see blue... And she is beautiful.

Eric Fuller
Belle Vernon, PA

Visitor in My Kitchen

A little baby gecko came to visit me today,
I screamed and yelled to let him know
There was no way he could stay.

He wasn't shy at all you see, coming right into my house,
A gnat or gecko I can handle
But not a snake or mouse.

He wasn't very big it's true, in inches two or three,
But when he scurried across the floor
He gave a fright to me.

Can I hit him with my shoe, I thought; I'll have to move fast,
When I share this with my friends tonight
They'll surely be aghast.

My shoe never fazed him; my aim's not so great.
I'm still used to asking
It to be done by my mate.

Then I got my handy broom; I didn't give a care.
I gave a swipe and over he went
With his feet up in the air.

Now he had to go; that second round I'd won.
"I'm not here to play games," I said,
"This isn't any fun."

I hope he'll find his momma, but no more will I care.
My doors and windows must be closed
As my house I will not share!

Irma Wolfe
Sumter, SC

I'm learning what life is like to suddenly be a seventy-seven-year-old widow and realizing one must retain humor.

The Scent of Seasons

Cover your eyes and be sure and don't peek,
Summer's undressing for winter's long sleep,
Trees with their limbs uncovered and bare,
Are exposed to the elements each must share.

The fields are now empty and yellow with age,
Where corn once stood as actors on stage,
Erect—alert—ready for cue,
Now winter collects what is long past due.

Summer played with the autumn and flirted with cold,
Like a mouse in a cat's mischievous hold,
Now locked in the grip of prison's white,
Are summer's bright days caught in winter's bite.

Sparkling filled jars stood side by side,
Their smug gold mouths smiling so wide,
Locked away safely—yet in perfect view,
Was summer's reward and treasure, too.

A scent now and then from the freshly mowed hay,
Drifted in from the barn of the season's day,
The bales had been stored into each corner and space,
Signaling the end of the fervent race.

Lean back and sigh and rest a bit,
Meditate, nod and dream while you sit,
The stormy clouds will come—then go,
And seasons like tides, will ebb and flow.

Ramona J. Johnson
Canton, IL

A childhood vision of cellar shelves with the canned golden-ringed jars sitting neatly together inspired "The Scent of Seasons" poem. A severely ill mother of three children left the summer's canned fruits and vegetables to feed her children through the winter season. She sensed she would not live to be with them to do so. And so the memory lingers, even into an elderly age, of such a loving Christian mother.

What a Vacation

My wife went on vacation, and left me all alone.
A bowl of homemade noodles, and a handheld telephone.

When I got her to the airport, and she gave me one last look,
She said, "Sorry honey, you're going to have to cook."

My face looked long and peaked.
My heart was really torn.
My stomach said to itself, here comes that damn popcorn.

Her vacation is about over, but that isn't all;
She told me this morning she's going again next fall.

Those words never hurt me nor did they tear me apart, the only thing
That came out of me was another popcorn fart.

Larry Dressler
Tyler, TX

Grace

Hiking up a familiar trail
my boots crunched against bits
of wood and moist granular soil.
Quietly absorbing the fragrance
of Ponderosa pines and the peace of the forest,
the cares of the past week slipped away.
Streams of sunlight pierced layers of time.
Trees cast their shadows across the path.
Blue spruce stood alone as arrows
pointing to the sky.
Small aspen trees swayed back and forth
as the wind rustled through their branches.
As the path turned and twisted through the forest
a dull roar in the distance grew louder and louder.
White waters exploded in the sunlight,
crashed against rocks and boulders.
Strong currents changed the river's course,
shaping its contour.
Rocks and pebbles tossed and tumbled,
reshaped countless times.
Old thought patterns crumble
as rocks remolded by
the stream's relentless pressure.
Each moment new water replaces the old.
A hope for change.
Grace to start over.

Carol Bonney
Arvada, CO

Love: My Life Sentence

I didn't need a love so perfect in every way. I didn't need a
prince on a white horse. I just needed someone who would stay.
I didn't need a fairy tale romance, from where I came
anyone would be worth a chance. I wish there would've
been another way. I wish I was in a better place as I
stand here today. I always knew I would never replace,
all I ever see is your face. Another has taken my place.
Listened and hoped against hope they were right. Tried
everything to move on. I wanted to be wrong and believe
time heals all. A love that felt so natural there was nowhere
to go but to fall. They were so wrong. Tried to move on with
so many things now when this heart sings, such a different
song. There's a deep sadness, so different when we used
to sing such happiness. I was so vulnerable, you took advantage,
I resisted but you persisted and in time you won the dance.
I mistook your determination for real feeling. Either you
didn't know your own mind or were very cruel with no heart.
I try to get through the night but nothing again would ever
be right. I fought the fight it left me tired but my heart was
still my heart and it never stopped replaying the day you
said you wanted to part. I knew it would never change and
feel better. I knew that day I would always feel the same
way. No matter how I tried, this was one storm that I just
couldn't weather. Twenty years later and as raw as that fateful
day you walked away. My life sentence, loving you when you wanted
me to and unable to stop when you replaced me with someone new.

Alice Neilson
Herminie, PA

My inspiration for this poem was my own heartbreak many years ago and my experience dealing with lost love and unrequited love. I've learned a part of the heart is always lost and time doesn't heal all. I don't believe "'tis better to have loved and lost than never to have loved at all." Some will go their whole lives and just think they are in love. It's easy to go through the motions, never knowing any different but if you're lucky or sometimes unlucky, you will feel the difference and realize everything before was just pretending.

Enlightenment

Open my eyes and help me view
Each of the hearts in this room.

Open my heart help me to see
What is happening deep inside me.

Open my mind and bring it to light
To share the love with such delight.

Open my mouth cause me to speak
Of your infinite love that brings joy and peace.

Open my ears and let me hear
The words of wisdom as the time draws near.

Sheila Welch
Zephyrhills, FL

Absolute Fear

Today I've seen what my eyes cannot see.
I've seen my delusions, my fears absolute destruction,
separation of the one I love and my death.
The speed of pain sometimes is so slow,
aggravating what we have left of our self control.
I am a human that cannot control my own mind.
Why does this seem so sad?
Why are my delusions coming to life?
Fear is my life.
Delusions are my normal and when I look at myself,
I am the thing I am most afraid of.

Kayla Marie Riggs
Sharon, PA

A Mother's Prayer

Our Father who art in Heaven I give you thanks for giving me joy and happiness. I will teach my child to love and honor and respect and to know the meaning of life. I touch my stomach and feel the movement of my child; the thrill and excitement when it moves tells me I am to be a mother soon.
Our Father let this day and every day of life be always blessed with the warmth of your presence and may my child know the meaning of life and love.

Anna Gasparro
Yonkers, NY

Index of Poets

E

F

G

H

I

J

K

L

M

N

O

P

R

S